BOYVILLE

BOYVILLE

JOHN ELSTNER GUNCKEL

ISBN: 978-93-5614-323-4

Published: -

LECTOR HOUSE LLP
E-MAIL: lectorpublishing@gmail.com

The president talking to the newsboys.

BOYVILLE

A HISTORY OF FIFTEEN YEARS' WORK AMONG NEWSBOYS

BY

JOHN E. GUNCKEL

ILLUSTRATED

To the Newsboys of America, and their Friends
this book is respectfully dedicated

CONTENTS

Page

PART FOURTH

PART FIFTH

PART SIXTH

PART SEVENTH

LIST OF ILLUSTRATIONS

Page

"IF you are going to do anything permanent for the average man you have got to begin before he is a man. The chance of success lies in working with the boy and not with the man. That applies peculiarly to those boys who tend to drift off into courses which mean that unless they are checked they will be formidable additions to the criminal population when they grow older.

"No Nation is safe unless in the average family there are healthy, happy children.

"If these children are not brought up well they are not merely a curse to themselves and their parents, *but they mean the ruin of the State in the future.*"

PRESIDENT THEODORE ROOSEVELT.

PART FIRST

CHAPTER I.

On the corner of one of the principal thoroughfares, in a very large city, there was located, fifteen years ago, a small grocery store. In front of the building the enterprising owner displayed fruits, vegetables and other goods; articles that were particularly tempting to boys.

In a near-by cottage there lived a very bright boy, twelve years of age, and familiarly known to every one in the neighborhood, as Jimmy, the newsboy. And that meant a bad boy.

On the disappearance of an occasional apple, an orange, or if one of the fruit-stands was upset, it was declared that Jimmy did it. All fights around the corner originated from Jimmy.

So bad was this boy's reputation that every one in the ward, including several Sunday-school teachers, was kept busy looking for a favorable opportunity to give Jimmy, what they thought he deserved, "a good licking."

The groceryman was not slow in letting his customers know how bad Jimmy was.

He was kicked, lectured, preached to, and a dozen times a day was pushed off the corner.

He was abused because he annoyed men and women by his misbehavior.

No one ever stopped to ask this boy where he lived; what about his parents, his home life, or to see if there was really any good in him worth trying to develop. The bad was visible, and the people seemed to delight in their vain efforts to correct him by censures and kicks.

There was no question about Jimmy being bad, about as bad as any street-boy would become who had his own way, and, whose parents permitted him to go and come when he pleased, and to associate with bad company, particularly boys older than he was.

Jimmy was a leader of a gang of little toughs who always met at the corner, in the evenings, and delighted in making it unpleasant for those who lived within hearing distance. He was strong, quick, and could throw to the ground any boy of his size, and never hesitated trying a much larger boy. He was the terror of the corners.

Yet with all his bad reputation, no one ever caught him doing anything for which he could be punished under the state laws.

Circumstantial evidence was all the groceryman could produce at any time he was accused. The boy who "squealed" to the groceryman about Jimmy had to remain away from the corner until he thought that Jimmy had forgotten it.

Jimmy was a typical newsboy.

He was not happy in fine clothes. He did not use the many slang phrases which so frequently become a part of a street-boy's life and enjoyment, but he had everything else.

He had a small route, perhaps thirty customers, for morning and evening papers, and when he had delivered his papers, he would hasten down town, get a new supply of the latest editions, and join the boys in selling on the streets.

He was an early riser, like all carriers, and long before the neighbors thought of getting up he was out on the street, and in all kinds of weather.

The station agent from whom he procured his morning papers said: "There is not a more faithful boy in the city, from a business view. But he has to be served first. He has a way of his own in pushing ahead of the crowd and is always among the first on his route. He pays cash for what he gets, but still, he is a bad boy."

A gentleman who lived in the neighborhood, and frequently called at the grocery store, became interested in Jimmy. There was something naturally attractive about the boy. There was a twinkle of his black eyes that was really fascinating.

"I would like to see what is back of that activity," said the gentleman, one day to the groceryman.

One afternoon, late in the fall, the gentleman was standing on the corner waiting for a car when the groceryman called him.

"You said you would like to see what Jimmy, the newsboy, was made of. He is up to some mischief now. He just bought a sack of hickory-nuts, and I'll bet a cooky he is making some one unhappy."

Two blocks away was a large lot, with a high fence around it. Scattered about the lot were a dozen or more hickory trees. The gentleman saw Jimmy climb the fence, walk to the farther side of the lot, and when under a heavy foliaged tree he stood for some moments looking in every direction. Finally he began to scatter hickory-nuts under the tree. Very carefully seeing that they were dropped all around this particular tree. Sometimes he would take a handful of leaves and cover over a lot of nuts. To the gentleman this was an unusual transaction, so he walked around to the big gate and followed a path across the heavy grass, and went to Jimmy.

"I have a curiosity to know what you are doing," said the gentleman, "and if you have no objections I would like to have you tell me."

Jimmy took him by the hand, that he might hasten towards the sidewalk, and when away from the tree, he said.

"You see, mister, termorrow is Saturday. There's no school. Across the street lives a whole lot of little boys and girls, and some of the boys don't like me very well, but that doesn't cut any figure with me. They comes over here every day after school and particularly on Saturday and hunt for hickory-nuts; but these old trees don't bear any more; they's dead. But that one over there, with the leaves, sometimes has hickory-nuts, but this year nary a nut is on the old tree. So I bought these here nuts an' scattered 'em all around the ground, an' termorrow I'll sneak around the fence and watch the girls an' boys gather them. Won't they be happy?"

"I should think they would," replied the man.

"They are real hickory-nuts, too," added Jimmy, "I blowed in fifteen cents at our grocery store. If you want to you may come termorrow an' I will guarantee you will see the happiest bunch ever gathered under a hickory-nut tree. Will you come?"

"Well, I should be delighted to come; and I will be there before you will," replied the gentleman kindly.

"You see," said Jimmy, "I cannot come until I deliver all my papers, an' that'll be about eight o'clock. If you get there before I do, don't you ever tell who put the nuts under the tree, will you?"

"I promise you, Jimmy, I will not only keep it to myself, but I will not even go on the lot, until you come."

A few words about Jimmy and his home, and they parted as friends.

"Under the hickory-nut tree termorrow there'll be a dozen happy girls an' boys, an' some of the boys don't like me," rang in the ears of the gentleman all during the evening and frequently in the night.

What a sermon, sowing and reaping.

"I am scattering hickory-nuts under this old tree for the children
to find termorrow."

See Page 2

CHAPTER II.

Saturday morning was an ideal autumn day; a day children delighted to go into the woods after hickory-nuts.

A few moments before eight o'clock the gentleman was slowly walking around the great lot when he saw Jimmy running at full speed down the street towards him.

Under the great trees were a dozen little boys and girls, and the air was filled with their merry laughter as they excitedly gathered into their baskets the hickory-nuts that Jimmy had so kindly dropped for their pleasure and happiness.

"They tell me, Jimmy, you're a bad boy," said the gentleman as they sat on a stump of a tree, in sight of the children.

Jimmy made no reply.

"Well, I don't care what any one says," added the gentleman, "I don't believe it. Your little act with the hickory-nuts has taught me a lesson I never learned in books. No boy would do that unless he has some good qualities in him. I feel honored to have this privilege of seeing those children so happy this morning, and to think who did all this. Jimmy," and he took his little hand in his, "I want you to make me a promise—I want you always to be my friend. What do you say?"

This was something Jimmy never heard of before. He was accustomed to being kicked, and censured, and for a man to ask him to be a friend was, what he afterwards called, "a new deal."

"Sure thing, I will," he said frankly.

"Now I want you to come down to my office, Monday after school, and we will talk over something that I want you to do for me."

"I'll be there," replied Jimmy, and after a moments thought he asked.

"And can I bring some of my friends with me?"

"Certainly, that is exactly what I want you to do. Bring your gang, all your friends, particularly the little toughs, and when you come into my office don't let any one stop you from seeing me."

"Oh, don't be afeared o'that, we knows as how to get there."

A few other things were talked about and they separated for the day.

As the gentleman rode down town he thought of the events of the morning, of the life of a newsboy. These little wiry, nervous street boys, alert of eye, and lithe of limb, who flock the principal thoroughfares of our great cities at almost all hours of the day.

Newsboys and bootblacks, boys whom the world seems to have forgotten. By peculiar conditions these boys are used to being at odds with the world. It need not be told that our newsboys, as a general rule, as people know them, are regarded as a swearing, stealing, lying, dishonest lot of young criminals, and these qualifications are recognized adjuncts to their business. With these conditions is it not a wonder that any of them ever succeed in working their way into the ranks of respectibility? People who curse and kick them, as they did Jimmy, never stop to think that these neglected newsboys, of today, sharp, shrewd and keen, may be the thieves, the burglars, the highwaymen; or the successful patriotic citizens of tomorrow.

No one will dispute the fact that, the street-boy is surrounded on every hand by degraded and vicious men, with drunkenness regarded as a desirable condition, and the indulgence in drink only limited by the ability to procure it.

Among many, robbery is regarded as a fine art, and the tribute of praise bestowed upon rascality. If christian people do not find time, amid the rush and roar of the city, in their mighty struggle for wealth, to lend a hand to lead him out on the highway of honest success, what is to become of the street-boy?

Is it not true that many a boy is bad because the best part of him was never developed?

It is not that a newsboy is so much worse than other boys, but simply that the other half of him didn't get a chance.

If you, dear reader, will take time to get into the real life of a boy, as the gentleman did with Jimmy, you will be surprised, as he was, at what you will discover. How quick he is to see an opportunity to do something bad, and when discovered, his conscience brings the blush of shame to his cheeks. Take boys like Jimmy, the leader of a gang of toughs, his acts on the public highway, his language, his ragged clothes all indicating neglect and evil designs, yet get his friendship, his confidence, and he will prove, as did Jimmy, the best and most faithful friend you ever had, not only in his youth, in his teens, but long after you have forgotten him.

No matter how bad the boy is, how miserable his environment, that great spark of good, that something, no one can explain its power, its influence, is still there. To get into touch with that life, to draw out the goodness of heart and make it a tangible blessing to the boys of our land, is the work every man and woman ought to try to do. It was this object the gentleman had in asking Jimmy and his friends to meet at his office. He felt that opportunities of this nature come but once in a life time.

George Eliot wrote: "The golden moments in the stream of life rush past us and we see nothing but sand. The angels come to visit us and we only know them when they are gone. How shall we live so as at the end to have done the most for others and make the most of ourselves." We become good ourselves only in the measure that we do good to some other soul. In Jimmy, the newsboy, no one stopped to see what was sleeping under the cover of extreme mischievousness. They were always looking for bad and they found it. Neglect is the mother of more calamities than any other sin, and who are neglected more than the newsboys?

CHAPTER III.

On the following Monday morning, at the appointed, hour, Jimmy, with eight other boys, was at the office of his newly-made friend.

It was an interesting picture, an exciting scene.

Noisy, loud talking, several answering questions at the same time, some turning over books, papers, investigating everything in sight. Sharp, shrewd, busy at every moment, quick to answer any question and the replies always satisfactory, and to the point.

"Don't you know anything," said Jimmy to a friend, who was trying to investigate how a typewriter was made, "let that meechine alone."

It was soon in evidence that Jimmy's word meant something, for each boy obeyed him without saying a word, except a little grunt of dissatisfaction, to show he hated to obey. Not one of the eight boys had clean hands. Not one a coat with a button. Three safety-pins held holding positions in some of their coats. Not one used a handkerchief, and the slang would puzzle many a lawyer.

As one of the boys lost his cap he said: "Some kid five-fingered it. — took it with his hand." It was an interesting crowd.

"Well, you are on time, Jimmy, and I see you have brought some of your friends with you," said the gentleman.

"These is part of de gang," said Jimmy.

"Do you boys all want to be my friends, just the same as Jimmy is?"

They replied, "Sure thing; cert. Yes'm."

These friendly words brought the gang closer to the gentleman's desk. And more papers were disturbed. The ink was investigated and one of the boys wanted to know why it wasn't red ink. Another poked his finger in the ink stand and made black streaks down the smallest boy's face. The gentleman was shown quite a number of articles they had in their pockets. Nails, buttons, marbles, pieces of slate-pencils, etc., all of which had to be admired.

"Say, you, mister," said a nine-year-old dirty-faced, bright-eyed boy, "I had trouble gittin' here. De con. wus onto me an' I had to take two lines 'fore I rode into de office wid out blowin' in a cent."

"Well, quit your wasting words," said Jimmy.

The boys gathered around the gentleman, and he said:

"My! what good you boys can do in this world with all of your push, and energy, your hustling, your good health, you boys can turn up something, and I'm going to help you do it. How would you like to help me make all the men and women who buy papers of you learn to love you. Learn to speak kindly to you?"

"Aw, de peoples don't care fur us." said a boy Jimmy called "Indian."

The original charter members.

See Page 8

"Well, I don't know about that. There is one thing certain there can be no harm in trying. The trouble is, people don't know you, and you won't let them get acquainted with you. Let's make a start. First, I want to know if every one of you wants to be a friend of mine? You do, that's a good start. And whenever you see me on the street, it doesn't make any difference what I am doing, or who I am talking to, will you come to me and say, good morning or good evening?" They all agreed.

"And another thing, when you boys are down town and should you hurt yourself, or get into some trouble, lose your papers, your money, or some one frightens you, I want you to call on me, and I will try to help you. Notice, I say when you are in trouble, because when you are doing well and everything comes your way, you need no assistance. You can take care of yourselves. What do you say, boys, to this?"

They all promised and were glad of the opportunity.

This was the first intimate talk with the gang.

Two days later, while the gentleman was very busy in his office, into the room came one of the little visitors followed by some of the gang, he was limping and crying as if his heart would break. He paid no attention to any one in the office but made directly for the gentleman, who seeing him, excused himself from his business friends and said to the boy,

"Well, now, what has happened to you?"

"A man shoved me off de sidewalk into de gutter and me foot struck a piece of glass," he replied, between sobs. His foot was bloody, and the more blood he saw the louder became his cries. He was taken into a near-by hotel, his foot carefully washed, a handkerchief tied over the wound, his tears wiped away, and when back into the office he said:

"I thank you, sir."

He picked up his bundle of papers, all pain had disappeared, the smiles again came to his pretty face, and with his friends, left the office, singing a popular air.

The result of this little act of duty added fifty new friends.

CHAPTER IV.

A week later, a little colored boy entered the office crying. He was known on the street as Midnight.

"Tree boys trowed me down in de alley, an' swiped me papers."

Four boys came with him. They wondered what would be done. While talking with him, Jimmy dropped in. Not quietly but made everybody get out of the way.

"I know the three kids," said Jimmy, "and I'll go after them."

So Jimmy left on his own accord. In fifteen minutes he returned bringing two boys.

"There, you kids," he said, "give Midnight back his money fur de papers you stole."

It was done. Midnight's eyes resumed their natural brightness, and he left happy, thankful to Jimmy for his interest.

To the gentleman this was a revelation. The power one boy can have over a gang of boys ought to be used for good. Such vital energy, such quick action, such nerve and endurance, all this must be used for doing good, for helping each other. My! what a boy who has influence among his fellow companions, can do. If each boy could be placed on his honor, each boy aiming to do the best he can to uplift his associate, trying to correct the little evils from which spring so many crimes, how much happiness, how many useful lives would result. If men would try to instill into the young hearts of our boys, our newsboys, because they are tempted more than any other class, a spirit of trust and love, instead of a spirit of fear and hate and revenge, what a happy unselfish world we would have. Suppose these newsboys, the boys who are so often accused of being bad, would be treated as Christ treated wrong-doers, not as criminals, but as misdirected and misguided boys, putting everything in their way to encourage them to do right. Suppose they were warned of danger, were propped up when about to fall, and personal efforts were made to find the good in each boy and to cultivate it as a husbandman would his garden—pulling out and destroying the weeds, removing the germs of disorder, and keeping a watchful eye over all even until the ripening of the fruit. What would be the result? The gentleman gave the subject considerable thought and concluded to try the experiment.

From the material at command it was surprising how many little good things sprung up where least expected and from soil considered as absolutely worthless. Like some products of the garden, good came from unexpected places.

Taking advantage of conditions and circumstances, the number of friends increased so rapidly that when cold weather set in, over a hundred little hustling friends of the street were added to the list.

Winter came with snow and ice and cold winds, making it hard for the carriers to deliver their papers before the breakfast hour. The little sellers were heard only a short time after the newspaper editions were out, and they were compelled to seek warm places. It was noticeable that the saloons of the city were the only places open to these boys seeking shelter and warmth.

There were several gentlemen in the city heartily in sympathy with the new movement among the newsboys, and among them was a generous clothier who presented, through the gentleman, fifty overcoats to be given to the poorest newsboys.

To select fifty of the most deserving, for the entire hundred were in want, was a very difficult task, especially as those interested had but little experience with boys of the street.

But Jimmy came to the rescue and he and the gentleman began to deliver the coats. When forty-five coats were given there remained twenty boys who were equally as needy as the others and there were but five coats left. How to select five boys from this number was the question.

Jimmy accomplished it.

The next day the gentleman was asked to go into the alley in the rear of the post-office where he met about sixty boys. Twenty of the poorest, those whose names were booked for coats, were asked to "stand in line against the building." Jimmy asked them to name five of their number who were very poor.

"You see, Kids," said Jimmy, "we have only five coats and if you select the five boys needing them it is all right."

The boys quickly named the lucky sellers.

Midnight, Peanuts, Bluster, Swipsey and Bundle were unanimously chosen and the orders were given to them.

This was a great surprise to the gentleman, for what he had imagined would be a difficult problem was satisfactorily settled in a very few moments by the boys.

"Boys, come close to me," said the gentleman. It was difficult for him to stand as they crowded so closely around him.

"I am surprised at your way of doing business. This is one of the greatest things I ever saw. It shows you boys can take care of yourselves and I believe you could manage worse things than dividing up a lot of coats. For this nice little act of yours I am going to give you a first-class Christmas dinner—"

Not another word could be heard. That quiet, listening bunch of boys was quickly changed to a turbulent, noisy crowd.

Several policeman came into the alley to see the cause of the noise. It wasn't common everyday cheering, but yelling. The invitation was accepted—it seemed by a thousand voices.

"All right, boys, get your little friends and meet me at the post-office steps Christmas morning at eleven o'clock."

"Say, Mister," said Swipsey, a bootblack, "only sellers and bootblacks in this deal?"

"Yes, only sellers and bootblacks this time, and I don't want a good boy in the crowd. I want only boys who are bad. I want all the gang and their friends. I want poor boys, but they must all be newsboys. That is, they must sell papers or shine shoes, and not a boy must come in dress suit."

Ready to start for the first Christmas dinner.

See Page 15

CHAPTER V.

Christmas morning came without a cloud in sight. The sun was warm. It was an ideal Christmas day. The boys were to meet at eleven o'clock, but fifty newsies were playing around the corners of the post-office as early as seven o'clock and at ten o'clock they came in groups of five and ten from every direction. When the gentleman appeared he was considerably embarrassed at the noisy reception. The boys formed in line by twos and as the hundred and fifty marched down the street yelling at the tops of their voices the good people of the city stood on the sidewalks wondering what had broken loose. The boys when near their destination, arriving at the top of a hill, without warning made a break for the bottom, like a flock of sheep scattering down a hill. They ran screaming as only boys can. At the door of the building, where they were to have their Christmas dinner, they were met by six policemen, who held them at bay, requiring them to go up stairs single file.

The tables presented a sight that even grown people considered, "one of the most attractive layouts ever seen in the city."

Flowers, fruit of all kinds, with "a mountain of turkey" and candy "to burn," greeted the boys. In just five minutes after the newsies were seated there was not an orange, an apple, a banana or a piece of candy in sight. All disappeared as if by magic. Ice cream and pie were first to receive attention. Turkey and chicken were later in demand. In half an hour the tables were cleared of everything that looked good to eat. Not only were the pockets of the boys filled with oranges and apples but their shirt-waists and pant-legs were bulged out with the things that pleased them most. Only six fights were recorded worthy of notice.

An entertainment followed the dinner. It was the kind and character they could understand and appreciate. Interesting and earnest talks by newspaper representatives, were sandwiched between acts. The object of the gathering was well defined by the members of the press. Their gentleman friend wanted the sellers and bootblacks to start a Newsboys' Association. This was received with the usual noisy approval. He wanted an association which the boys themselves would run; make their own laws, elect from their own numbers the officers, and everything connected with the running of the association to be under their supervision. On that Christmas day one hundred and two boys were enrolled in the new association, and their gentleman friend elected president, with Jimmy as vice-president.

The president was requested "to get busy," and, "prepare rules an' such things as we can work by."

After this meeting, Jimmy's friend was known as "Mr. President."

PART SECOND

CHAPTER VI.

A dozen or more newsboys can be seen at almost any hour of the day, dodging here and there around the corners, down alleys, or playing in the rear of the circulating offices of the great dailies. In all kinds of weather they will be found at their posts, prompt in delivering their papers to subscribers, or upon the streets crying the most important of the many head lines of the transactions of a day. Would it be possible to get this noisy, hustling crowd of boys together and gradually to bring this great power, this great force, into a channel for doing good? To form an association where the boy would be "de whole thing" with only the hand of man to guide where it was necessary? To simply push the button? In short, would it result in doing good among the class of boys who are neglected in more ways than men and women imagine? Reflection resulted in adopting a name that would imply everything—

"Boyville."

It means work with and among newsboys by the boys themselves.

The Boyville Newsboys' Association.

It was at once organized, and in its preamble of incorporation was written the Golden Rule. In the formation of Boyville it must not be understood that its mission was to draw good boys from good homes; but rather to give help to bad boys, come from where they may, when they appear on the streets—away from home influences. Whether they come from the most palatial residences on the shaded avenues, or from the crowded hovels of alleys, from poorly kept tenements, or even those who are compelled to sleep in public stairways, barns, or wherever a boy can creep under shelter without being noticed.

With one hundred and fifty-two newsboys, sellers and bootblacks, enrolled as active members for life; with an unwritten constitution and laws that were made to suit conditions, and that were subject to change at every meeting; with meeting places in alleys, in vacant store-rooms, theatres or wherever boys could meet on short notice, Boyville was started. Trustees were chosen from newspaper representatives, and leading citizens, but the detail work, the real work among the boys, was placed in the hands of the president—to make a success or failure of the project. It was first found necessary that the president should keep in personal daily touch with every boy, not in bunches but each boy, sellers and bootblacks. A membership card was issued. This card simply let the public know the bearer was a member of Boyville, Newsboys' Association. For this, and all benefits of the association, the boy paid nothing in money. No assessments of any kind. Nothing that would permit even a donation. He was simply required to obey the rules—

not to swear, to steal, to play craps, a game so common among sellers, or smoke cirgarettes.

Where the Boyville Newsboy's Association was organized, December 25, 1892.

See Page 15

There were but three officers, the president, vice-president and secretary. The two latter, newsboys. Jimmy the newsboy, and Johnny the bootblack, both leaders of gangs. These two boys were told that the success of the association depended entirely on their work. They had charge of the one hundred and fifty-two members. Their first orders were: "that each boy must watch the other boys and correct a fellow member for doing anything that would disgrace the association. They must not wait to see an officer to punish a member for stealing, swearing or playin' o'craps. They must not depend on what they heard, but on what they saw. Take the law into their own hands, and punish on the spot."

The end of the first month found twenty-eight membership cards taken from boys who had violated the rule, "you must not steal," and nine taken from boys who smoked cigarettes. The fines were from five to fifteen days. When the fines numbered fifty membership cards, the president made arrangements with a theatre to admit the members, permitting no boy to enter unless he showed his membership card. The boys who were fined, and did not have their cards, were dealt a pretty heavy blow, for boys. A little banquet was given and again no boy admitted to the hall without showing his card. This occasional hit had its effect in reducing the cards in the hands of the president to an average of about ten a month.

CHAPTER VII.

The membership increased so rapidly and the detail work became so extended, that it was found necessary to increase the number of officers, from two boys to eleven. The constitution and by-laws provided a Central Association, which was officered by boys who had experience upon the streets, as sellers and carriers. The vice-president gradually became familiar with the objects of the association, and the work among the boys. He was a typical newsboy, a good street-seller and his power was felt among the boys, especially those who were inclined to be bad. A secretary was elected from the ranks of the carriers. He was a good worker. The treasurer was a boy who received the unanimous vote of the association. The money he received was small donations, from benevolently-inclined friends. This was used for purchasing flowers for sick boys, etc. The real work of the association depended upon the executive committee of five members. Like most organizations, the committee-work centered in the chairman. The chairman of this committee proved to be one of the most active and faithful boys of the association. He left nothing undone in his efforts to unravel a difficulty or in correcting and building up a boy who had done wrong. The four boys on his committee were untiring in their efforts for the success of the association. This committee was in constant touch with the president.

The membership committee of three boys looked after old as well as new members. Each applicant had to be submitted to them for approval.

With these eleven officers, all boys under fourteen, the association began life. The constitution and by-laws embraced in its power and force simply one aim, one object, to do good among the boys. To do it effectively, and make the results lasting. To build up, never pull down; to encourage honesty, to watch and warn a boy.

The work among the street boys became more interesting as the months rolled on, and, at the end of a year the membership of Boyville had increased to two hundred and fifty sellers and bootblacks. This number not only included boys who sold papers every day, but those who sold extras, and on Saturdays, and special occasions, and boys who sold magazines or other periodicals. The association began to grow and become recognized by the boys generally, and new sellers appeared upon the streets daily, all anxious to join. The working officers remained the same—but two boys doing the detail work.

Two years passed under the new officers and rules. The Boyville Newsboys' Association began to be felt in the community. Compliments were frequent concerning the good work. The association had increased its membership to fifteen hundred and twenty boys. A little army, and all working harmoniously together for each others good, and in trying to assist and build up the association. Doubting men and women, and the world is full of them, were perfectly satisfied of the success of the boys governing themselves, as was shown almost daily in the work. The boys solved a problem never thought of being tried by men and women who had long experience in working among boys.

The success of Boyville increased in proportion to the work done by the young officers.

People began to look upon a newsboy with some consideration, and as a necessary adjunct to the growth of a city. His politeness, his honesty, his general deportment attracted special notice, and the boys received many kind words and increased attention.

The association began to assume such magnitude that it was found necessary to divide it into auxiliaries, to get a suitable badge, and a membership card defining more explicitly certain rules.

Boyville was therefore divided into five auxiliaries—the sellers, north, south, east and west branches, with the constitution of the Central. Each auxiliary had eleven officers, making a total of sixty-six officers—all boys. In the annual election of officers great interest was taken by the boys, many displaying political "wire pulling" qualifications that would equal the work done by great political bodies.

These sixty-six officers were scattered in all parts of the city, making it almost impossible for a boy whom they wanted for violating a rule of the association, to escape their notice.

The membership card told the story of what was expected of a member. It is herewith given for that purpose.

No. — — — — —

THIS IS TO CERTIFY THAT

— — — — — — — — — —is an active member for life of The Boyville Newsboys' Association. He does not approve of swearing, lying, stealing, gambling, drinking intoxicating liquors, or smoking cigarettes, and is entitled to all the benefits of said association, and the respect and esteem of the public.

Signed by the officers.

With these rules, and simple pledge, if pledge it can be called, in the hands of each newsboy, the reader can imagine the good that must result.

It does not say the holder is guilty of any of these evils, neither does it imply that he must not swear, etc., but it does say, and each boy is strongly impressed with the fact, that he does not approve of these things, and will not permit a fellow member to violate a single rule.

A boy who says I do not believe in swearing, while he may swear himself, will take great pleasure in checking some one else, and often bumps up against a strong proposition when he finds some other boy, probably of greater strength, watching him, and waiting anxiously for an opportunity to correct him. If not corrected with a simple warning it may end in a fight.

A bunch of sellers.

See Page 20

A boy makes an application for membership. He is recommended by a friend. He is approved by the membership committee. In case there is something wrong with the applicant, particularly if he steals, or swears, or smokes cigarettes, he is sent with a note to the president, or as is more frequently done, one of the officers reports in person giving the president a history of the applicant and the failing he has.

The new member knows nothing of this, in fact he gives expression to his thoughts and says, after he receives his credentials, "It's dead easy." It is, as far as the business he has with the president, but the moment he leaves the president's office, the officers living in his district are notified of the trouble this boy gives, or bad habit he delights in keeping up.

Even the boys with whom he associates become familiar, through methods of their own, with his failings, and go after him with all the authority of an official.

With all the interest taken by the boys to correct a member for violating one of the rules, and the severe methods adopted by them to correct a known evil, it is seldom a boy will appear against one of his associates as a witness.

A gentleman whose sympathy was with the work, brought a boy to the president whom he accused of using language, "unbecoming a criminal." As witnesses he brought with him four newsboy companions.

Imagine the gentleman's surprise to hear the boys say: "Mister, you're dreaming through a pipe. He didn't swear." The boys did not even show signs of embarrassment but faced the charge with perfect ease. No argument could get the boys to testify against their friend.

The gentleman left disgusted with newsboys.

"I will let you boys settle this among yourselves," said the president.

They went upon the street, into the alley. Half an hour later the newsboy accused of swearing returned. Timidly he approached the president and said.

"I swore but I will never do it again, and I mean it, I am sorry."

At the door the president saw four little faces peeping through the window. They were watching their friend.

"Where is your badge?" asked the president.

"The boys took it from me, they're out there," he replied.

They were beckoned to come in.

"Did you do the right thing?" one of the boys asked the accused.

"Yes, didn't I Mr. President?" he answered, looking for sympathy.

"Yes, boys, he is all right. I understand everything," said the president.

The badge was returned to the boy and they left the office talking and laughing.

CHAPTER VIII.

The first public appearance of the boys, aside from auxiliary meetings, annual Christmas dinners, attending theatres, entertainments, base-ball games, picnics, etc., and where the boys made a favorable impression upon the public, was the Sunday afternoon meetings held in suitable halls, during the winter season. These were carried on successfully and profitably for several years, until the available halls were too small to accommodate the increasing membership.

The idea of Sunday afternoon meetings suggested itself from what the boys said.

"If we had meetings of our own we would not attend Sunday afternoon theatres." Three boys, newsboys, were seen coming out of the back door of a saloon on Sunday afternoon, and to the question asked by the president, why they spent their time in the saloon, they replied they had no other place to go to get warm.

"Why not go home?"

"We are not wanted at home."

At the Sunday afternoon meetings the entertainments were given by the different Sunday schools of the city, and occasionally by some society, all kindly volunteering their valuable services. Splendid music, interesting talkers, little girls and boys in recitations or songs who always made a hit among the newsies. In time the newsboys became so interested in the work that many of them concluded that they could "do a stunt or two," and the program was divided in two parts. First, the Sunday-school or society, followed by the newsboys who introduced their best speakers, singers, etc.

"These Sunday afternoon gatherings," to copy from an editorial in one of the daily newspapers, "have improved the tastes, aroused the better natures, stimulated the ambitions, revealed new and nobler ideals and altogether, have opened a new world of more sober and serious plans for future success of the bright little business men."

One of the most trying incidents that ever came to the attention of the president was at one of the Sunday afternoon meetings held in a theatre, when was brought to the rear of the stage two newsboys so drunk that a policeman had to hold them from falling.

They had a bottle of whiskey between them. In broken sentences they told where a keeper had sold them the liquor, Sunday morning, and how the men in the saloon dared them to drink all the whiskey in the bottle. It wasn't necessary to drink all, a few swallows made them dizzy. "We got funny and noisy, an' the man pitched us out." They staggered towards the opera house to attend the newsboys' meeting, when a policeman assisted them in the house. Immediately upon their entrance their friends hustled them out of sight behind the stage. The president at once called the association officers and turned the two boys over to them. Quickly the officers removed their badges. It was difficult to restrain some of them from "giving the boys a thorough thrashing." Through the influence of the boy, Jimmy, the sympathy of the newsboys' turned quickly to the two boys and a determination for revenge on the saloon keeper followed. The newsboy officers took the two little fellows to their homes. In a few days they reported to the president that the boys received such a severe punishment from their parents that they would be laid up for a month. The saloonman was visited by two of the oldest experienced officers. They were received with kindness, and after talking over the matter for some time it was mutually agreed that the boys were to notify all members that they must keep out of the saloon, as the proprieter promised not to sell liquor of any kind to newsboys and to refuse to sell liquor to any of the fathers of the news-boys—"when he thought they had enough."

For a month the boys watched that saloon, and if a newsboy entered, his badge was taken from him. The saloonman took greater interest than the boys, for he absolutely refused to sell liquor to any one whom he thought had "all he could carry."

Today this saloonman is respected by the newsboys and many good deeds are credited to him.

"He is simply trying to lift up a man instead of pulling him down," said an officer.

The good that has been accomplished from the Sunday afternoon meetings, commonly called "The Popular Sunday School," cannot be estimated. Thousands of people attend these meetings. They are pleased because the newsboys do the entertaining. There isn't a great deal of preaching, but there is enough. "The object is not to give so much of that sort of thing," says an editorial in one of the great dailies, "but what preaching they get is wholesome. The boys get a chance to laugh and clap their hands. They are permitted to be boys on Sunday just as on week days. There is good music, too. It is apt to be a patriotic air, or a popular song. A sweet little girl sang 'The Good Old Summer Time,' and the newsies joined in the chorus. It wasn't classical, but it was good. Instead of shooting over people's heads the musicians aim at their hearts. The preaching isn't a tiresome string of 'does' and 'don'ts,' 'musts' and 'mustn'ts'. It is mostly plain talks from plain peo-ple who know they are talking to boys whose veins are bulging with rich, red human blood. But the boys themselves furnish most of the program. Boys who sell papers, who shine shoes, on the streets, get up before big audiences, make speech-es, sing songs, 'recite pieces' and do other interesting and instructive stunts. And hundreds of these little newsboys sit in the auditorium, conduct themselves like gentlemen and thoroughly enjoy the entertainment. An interesting fact about this association, is that its membership comprises the rich as well as the poor. If a rich man's son carries a route he is in the same boat with the poorest lad that peddles papers on the street. There are boys who have rich fathers, boys who have poor fathers, boys who have industrious fathers, boys who have drunken fathers, and boys who have no fathers at all. There are Protestant boys, Catholic boys, Hebrew boys, white boys, black boys—and all are full-fledged, honored members of the same newsboy family, which is run on the principle of equal rights for all and special privileges for none. Rich boys are not debarred. There is a desire to save them from wealth's temptations and make good citizens of them in spite of their handicap. The poor boys who sell papers to help keep the family from starvation are generous and are willing to let the rich in on the ground floor. So it is a pretty broad and big Sunday-school. And a good one. Every boy who belongs to it is better for his membership. He is taught to travel on his own merits and not lean on his papa. He is taught that he must paddle his own canoe; and that he will be judged by what HE does, not by his father's success."

Festival Hall.
Where the National Newsboy's Association was organized, August 16, 1904.

See Page 29

CHAPTER IX.

So great became the interest in the success of the Boyville Newsboys' Association that many additions were made to add to its prosperity, through which the association became favorably known throughout the United States.

A newsboys' band of thirty-eight pieces was organized, the sellers being in the majority. The expense of the band was borne entirely by one of the enterprising dailies. The musical talent, discovered by an efficient leader, in the newsboys, was remarkable. In less than a year they were able to play some of the most difficult pieces, and the general deportment of the boys surprised all who saw them.

The organization of the South-end Cadets was an event which proved to be one of the most successful additions to the association. Their fine personal appearance, their remarkable drilling, their good behavior at all times and on all occasions, with the band, made Boyville extensively and favorably known as the home of the best newsboys in the world.

Nothing in the history of the work among the newsboys was as important as the interest taken by the various churches, regardless of sect, through their ministers, in holding special Sunday evening meetings for the members of the association. All through the city the auxiliaries were invited, and particular pains taken in the preparation of a program suitable to all. When the boys were first invited, the expression was frequently heard: "Gee wiz, we gets front rows." The illustration shows the boys marching to one of these evening entertainments.

The value of these meetings cannot be estimated. The good attendance, the close attention, the good behavior of the boys made them many friends, and people began to look more kindly upon the newsboy.

With these improvements in the street-boy and the success of the association naturally, the president received many letters from men and women all over the land seeking information about the detail work of the association.

With the view that this work may eventually be extended throughout the country, the president conceived the idea that a convention of newsboys and their friends might be held and a National association organized through which much good could be accomplished. He therefore opened correspondence with the managers of the World's Fair, St. Louis, Mo., with a view of getting their consent and approval to set apart a day to be known as Newsboys' Day. This met with prompt reply and a most hearty endorsement of the officials, and newspaper representatives generally throughout the United States, and resulted in selecting Tuesday, August 16, 1904, as Newsboys' Day.

That the convention might prove a success, particularly among men who are familiar with work among newsboys, the aid of the circulating managers of the newspapers was asked. At the annual convention of the National Association of Managers of Newspaper Circulation, held at the World's Fair June 12, 1904, the president of "Boyville" appeared and explained the methods adopted in this association. He satisfied them that, not only did the association accomplish much good, through its efforts to influence boy's work, but it also proved to be a great aid to the newspapers in increasing circulation. He therefore asked for endorsement and support of the members of this organization in forming a National Newsboys' Association.

In recognition of this a resolution was unanimously passed endorsing the movement; and a committee was appointed to co-operate with the trustees of the Boyville association with the view of not only making Newsboys' Day a success but in organizing a National Newsboys' Association.

CHAPTER X.

On the afternoon, of Tuesday, August 16, 1904, in the magnificent Festival Hall, at the World's Fair, where were present hundreds of newsboys, representing nearly every State in the Union; and newspaper representatives from the leading papers of the country, there was organized The National Newsboys' Association; officers were elected and instructions were given them to perfect the organization and adopt the plan so successfully carried on by the Boyville Newsboys' Association, and having for its object the extension of the work in every town and city in the land that there may be established fraternal relations among newsboys everywhere in making them an important part in the business world, honored and treated with respect by all good citizens.

While the details of the organization were being worked out, the officers were instructed, by the trustees, to issue membership cards and badges and to organize auxiliaries in cities and towns wherever desired.

A year has passed since the organization of the National Newsboys' Association, and the officers have established auxiliaries in many cities and towns in the United States with inquiries from foreign cities.

In the discussion regarding the formation of the constitution etc., it was agreed that an organized association of newsboys with an enrollment of twenty-five boys would be received into the National Association as an auxiliary, and, in towns where there were a less number than twenty-five newsboys, each boy could become members under the trustees of the National Association.

No recognition of the work accomplished by the National and Boyville Associations was so important and no greater good can be accomplished than the official approval and endorsement by the officers of the greatest railroads in America.

It is an undisputed fact, railroad detectives as authority, that a majority of the young men arrested for stealing merchandise from freight cars were once boys who sold or waited for newspapers at the stations of our railroads.

The officers of the Boyville Association have on file congratulatory letters from prominent railroad detectives heartily approving of the work accomplished in trying to teach the boys who sell or wait for papers at the stations, honesty. One detective wrote: "You are saving the railroads thousands of dollars worth of property and a million dollars worth of trouble."

The railroads who have approved of the work have permitted the officers of the National Association to issue circular letters to their agents instructing them to allow no newsboy to sell or wait for newspapers at the stations unless he is a member of the association and wears, while on duty, the official badge. This simply means that newsboys to sell or wait for papers at railroad stations must not swear, steal, lie, smoke cigarettes or gamble. The trustees, feeling that the good work accomplished among the newsboys would be still further advanced by bringing the National Association to public notice, decided that the expense of sending the newsboys' band and cadets to Washington, to take part in the inaugural parade of President Theodore Roosevelt on March 4, 1905, would be justified.

Correspondence with the inaugural committee proved one of the pleasant experiences, for the recognition by the chief marshall and other officials of the civic grand division was quickly and heartily given. The work of completing the detail arrangements, necessarily irksome, was so cordially conducted that the trustees felt more than ever justified in sending the newsboys' band and cadets, and the vice-presidents of the various auxiliaries, in order that Boyville could be officially represented.

"Sixty-five newsboys let loose in the city of Washington during the inaugural ceremonies would cause the men in charge more trouble and unhappiness, and disgrace to the city represented than the honor gained," was the public declaration of men who were not familiar with what could be done by newsboys.

Satisfactory arrangements were made in all details.

To show the activity and self-responsibility of a newsboy, while the boys were en route they stopped at Cleveland. Two hours were given them to go where they pleased. In less than an hour the sellers said:

"We have done the town, been all through the public buildings and we're ready to go. We were treated like reporters."

In Washington thirty minutes after their arrival at headquarters, the president called a dozen boys to him and tried to tell them how to find their hotel(?) from a given point.

"Aw, what you trying to give us. We ain't asleep. We've been round the square, and say, president, we found a first-class eating place. It's out o' sight."

Two hours after the boys were settled, a majority of them had been through and around nearly all of the public buildings, and were ready "to do the White House." When requested to report at a stated hour and place, every boy was there on time and to the minute.

One of the greatest lessons the president learned from the trip, from these newsboys, was the perfect control they have of themselves.

They were always happy. Always contented and satisfied with conditions. Never complaining or borrowing trouble showing that worry is a thing unknown to newsboys. The loss of a hat, of a piece of baggage, an order changing contemplated plans, all were received with the same wonderful patience and good cheer, which seem part of the nature of a newsboy. The boy without a cent in his pocket was happier than the boy whose parents supplied him with more money than he needed. Wherever these boys appeared on the streets of Washington they were little gentlemen, an honor to the city who sent them, an honor to themselves and, an honor to the great country they represent. On the train en route Governor Myron T. Herrick, in his address to the boys said: "I consider it a very great honor to the state of Ohio to send from its commonwealth such a bright lot of boys, and boys who represent our little street merchants, boys who are destined to be the good men of the future."

**Newsboys' Band and Cadets—ready to start for Washington, D. C.,
to participate in the inaugural parade of President Roosevelt, March 4, 1905.**

See Page 30

CHAPTER XI.

Newsboys are students. From the necessity of knowing the special happenings of the day, as soon as they receive their papers they quickly read the head lines. First, they can be seen to slowly spell each word, but in a very short time they read without assistance. It is one of the advantages to boys selling papers, it is an educator. To be successful, they must become familiar with the news of the day and be able to cry it to induce men to purchase.

After the inaugural parade, when most people were tired, the newsboys, at their headquarters, "chipped in" and raised enough money to send one of the boys "down town to purchase a copy of every paper sold in the city." The boy returned with New York, Philadelphia and Washington dailies and a dozen sellers were seated on the cots, each earnestly reading, and commenting on leading articles. One little seller said:

"Say, look here, fellers, Teddy has started to work, he made an appointment. I guess he means business."

Is there another organization whose members, when attending a convention, are so interested in the news of the day as to send one of their number — "down the avenue to purchase a copy of each of the dailies the town takes?"

From the highest officers in the land; from the committee in charge of the various divisions; from the foreign as well as the Washington newspapers, praise and compliments were given these newsboys for the almost perfect marching, in the parade.

They said:

"The newsboys' band and cadets made the hit of the day, in the parade, and made thousands of friends throughout the United States * * * President Roosevelt was immensely pleased with the newsboys and could not say enough of the remarkable appearance they made. The Newsboys' Band and Cadets, sixty-five in all, which led the third brigade of the civic grand division, are the first newsboys in America to be recognized in an inaugural parade. The band thirty-eight pieces, is uniformed in red with black trimmings; the cadets, twenty, with red and white trimmings. The cadets march under the leadership of Drum-Major Francis McGarry, the youngest drum-major in the world, and a little fellow who has to take a hitch-step every other step in order to keep up with the procession. The general appearance and manly conduct of the young gentlemen elicited many favorable comments. They were an object lesson of a very remarkable character, which is calculated to arouse in them a higher degree of patriotism and love for their country."

PART THIRD

"I am an officer of the sellers' auxiliary; get busy."

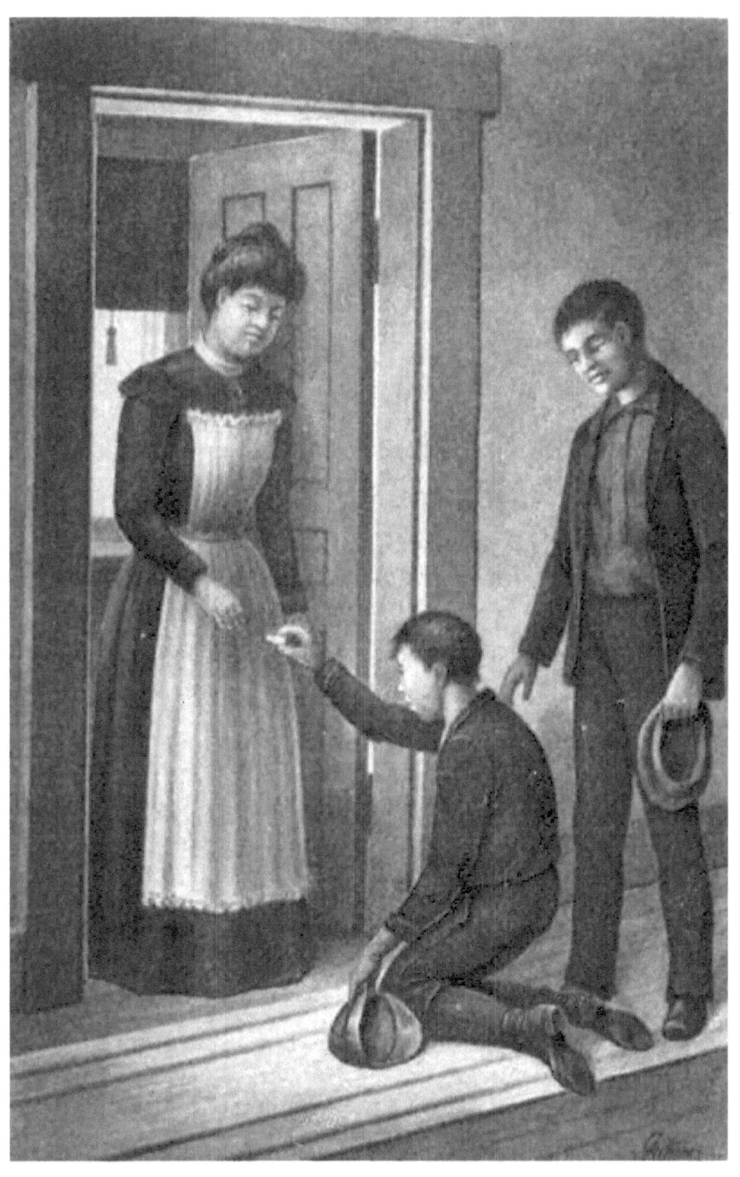

"Lady, I am sorry I run away wid de money."

See Page 37

CHAPTER XII.

The reader will observe that when Boyville was well organized no boys were admitted to membership except those who sold newspapers or shined shoes. But later, after many years of work, incident after incident came to the president of the wrong-doings of the carriers who occasionally sold extras. Those boys came from the best families and much was expected from them by the sellers. But some of them proved to be very bad boys. The following is one of a number of incidents that induced the president to include the carriers in the association.

A very kind lady, living in the heart of the city, and who was a subscriber to one of the dailies, reported to the president; "a boy who carried my paper and whom I owed eighteen cents, has skipped with a dollar. He did not have the change and asked permission to cross the street to get it. I saw him run down the street as fast as his little legs would carry him. I knew he was running away and would not return. It is not so much on account of the money, that I call your attention to this, as it is to correct the boy, and save him from future wrong doing."

She was asked to describe the boy. As it was dark this was difficult.

"But I did notice," she said, "that he had on a very bright pink necktie."

This was the first instance she knew of the boy being dishonest. He had always delivered the paper promptly, never missing a day.

"But, a big new dollar was too much for him."

Immediately upon the receipt of this information the president called his best officer and repeated the story.

"A pink necktie," he said. "Let me see, there is a pretty lively little fellow that comes down town occasionally and poses on the corners. I know him. He always wears that necktie."

Inquiry among the sellers soon gave the officer all the information necessary as to where the boy lived. He was not a member of the association. He was a carrier. He was supposed to be good. A dozen boys knew the pink necktie carrier.

Following is the official report of the officer who went after the boy.

"I found he lived over a mile from the place where he delivered the paper. It was a swell part of the city. When I went there I asked for the boy. He was in bed. I told his mother I wanted to see him on some very particular personal business. He was tucked up in a nice warm bed, and I hated to disturb him. When I asked him if he had received a dollar from a lady for papers, he covered his head with the clothes. I knew I was right. I told him to get out of bed, and go with me to see the lady, return her money, and beg her pardon. I had him dead to rights for he didn't want his mother to know what he had done. I went down stairs and told his mother I had some very important things we boys wanted him to do. She hesitated a little and finally let him go. He dressed, and when on the way I told him he must get down on his knees and beg the lady's pardon; he cried and said, 'I will go home before I'll do that.' All right, I said, if you want your mother to know what a little rascal you are, how you steal money, we'll go back, but if you want to be a little man, and make things right, with my help, well and good. When we reached the house, we had to go up a stairway, and the boy threw himself on the steps and said, 'Oh, I can't do this,' but I said you could steal all right, so come on. Up the stairs we went, and I knocked at the door. I thought that boy would faint. 'Oh, I can't do it,' he cried, when the door opened and the lady stood before him. She understood the situation. She lifted him to his feet. I pulled him back, and said, 'No, my lady, he must get down on his knees, return you the dollar, and beg your pardon.' It was a tough job for that kid, but he did it; and after it was all over he said, 'My! but I feel better, I'm glad this is over.' On the way he told me he had spent forty cents and had but sixty cents left to pay the lady, so I gave him the money to make the dollar, and he is to pay me five cents a week until all is paid up. On the way home he was the happiest lad I ever saw. The lady said it was the slickest piece of detective work she ever heard of, and wished to thank you and the boys for starting the association."

A few days after this little incident, the boy was brought to the president, by the officer, requesting that he become a member of Boyville. His name was signed to an application and when the officer asked him how he felt after returning the dollar, he looked a little ashamed, but quickly said: "You bet, I'll never do any thing like that again. It isn't safe in this city, the kids find a fellow out when they are bad. I'm glad we fixed it up all right."

He gradually paid back the money the officer advanced. Two years have passed since that eventful night, and today the boy is one of the most efficient officers in the Boyville association.

The following editorial is taken from one of the city dailies relative to the pink necktie story. It reads:

"The story explains how well the officer did his work. There is a lesson for boys and men, too, in this little story. It shows that policemen and jails are not necessary when boys and men know how to do right. No policeman, judge or jury was needed to straighten out this difficulty. Newsboy government did the work. It got the woman her money, and taught the boy with the pink necktie a lesson he will never forget. He didn't have to be arrested or go to jail. The public will never know who he is. He will not be further disgraced. Now, why do these boys, officers of this association, do this? simply because they are proud of the reputation of their association. They have learned that the association's reputation is made up of the reputations of its members. They have learned that one dishonest act by one newsboy reflects on all newsboys and on the organization. So they insist that all members must be honest and protect the association's good name. It isn't fear of the policemen or jails that makes these boys honest. It is the fear of their own conscience and the opinion of their comrades. They want to be able to walk along the street with their heads up, and to look every honest man squarely in the eye. They know they are as good as the richest man in town if they are honest. They are learning that it pays to do right, and not because of what may happen to them as a result of dishonesty. If men would follow the same plan the world wouldn't need its thousands of jails, reformatories and penitentiaries. If men would only feel that each one of them is a member of the human society, association or organization, and that wrong committed by one is a reflection on all, it would save heartaches and trouble in this world."

CHAPTER XIII.

Do you believe a boy that is good at home, one who is cared for and loved as we often see an only child, could possibly do anything bad on the streets, away from home influence?

A neatly dressed boy, a carrier, whose parents "wanted him to learn the trade of the street, to give him self-reliance and business tact, and all that the street teaches without much effort," when through with his little route of carrying papers insisted upon going, "to the heart of the city and selling papers on special occasions, extras."

Before Boyville was fully organized the president's attention was called to this little fellow—as being "a perfect nuisance. He was impudent, frequently used profane language and was one of the worst boys on the street." At that time the association had but one (boy) officer. He was told to watch this boy. See that he was corrected. "And, above everything not to lose him because he was bad." Within a month the officer reported "the boy's parents were among the best in the city, good Christian people, attending church every Sunday, and the boy a regular prize-winner for perfect attendance at Sunday-school. When this boy was away from home, out of sight of his parents—he was a little terror."

"Well, what did you do with him?" was asked the officer.

"I takes his papers, an' shows him as how to sell 'em. How to say thank you when he sells to a gemmen or a ladies. And how's not to be the whole thing when on the street working. He cut out swearing de furst thing. He was easy doing, all he wanted wus guidin."

"What did he say to your work?"

"When I puts twenty cents in his hand, an' says this is yourn, he gets wise, he gets next to a good thing and is now working on de square. He is de boss seller on de street an' no boy kin sell on de corners and swear, or steal. He fights 'em. He does."

That same little boy, who was given a warning by a fellow companion with a little authority, today receives a salary of eight hundred dollars a year in an important commercial position.

In every city of our land there are hundreds of boys like this "good boy at home," who on the street surprises their most intimate friends by their wickedness.

"Trow de cigarette away."

See Page 41

The newsboy cannot gain admission to many of the boys clubs, debating clubs, athletic clubs, and is often debarred from many of our greatest christian associations, because he is a being within himself, he stands alone in his class, a creation of his own acts and deeds, and goes upon the street at that age when environment molds his future, and generally molds it bad.

A question is often asked, what would become of a boy if he were left to himself, with no training, no guidance, no education. A boy of the street, who is dead to home influences, or worse, who is driven out to make a living for himself by heartless parents or guardians, or unfortunate conditions of life, and there are hundreds of them in every city, becomes a power in himself. For evil, first. "For the heart of the sons of men is fully set in them to do evil." If left alone the evil will get the upper hand. The street teaches irregular habits and restlessness.

The following incident will show how diligent were the boys, not officers, in watching their companions.

Two little boys, ages nine and twelve, saw a fellow member standing in an alley, behind a pile of store boxes and enjoying a cigarette to his great delight. He was afraid to appear on the street as the boys were watching for such cases. He was a boy about fifteen years of age, rather stout and independent, but a staunch member of the association. He might have used his strength to great advantage in arguing with the two boys who attacked him as soon as discovered.

"Say, Mike, youse knows it's agin the rule to smoke dem cig'rettes."

"Dat's all right. If I wants to smoke, I smoke, see? No one sees me in the alley. I don't smoke when I sells me papers."

"Aw! comes off, youse knows de rules. Cut it out. Trow it away. Youse knows our president don't wants youse ter smoke 'em. Cut it out. Trow it away."

This persuasive talk or "bluff" as the smoker declared, had but little effect until the two boys began to take off their coats. When donned for the prize ring, the boys walked to the violator, presenting a bold front and again demanded that the cigarette be thrown away, and promise made that he would never smoke again.

"What youse goin' to do?" he said, backing up closer to the building. "We will trow you down, take your badge frum youse an' take it to the president."

The big boy stood quiet for some moments, in the mean time about thirty newsies had gathered around him, each yelling—"trow it away."

"I haint lookin' fur no trouble," he finally said, and threw the cigarette in the alley.

"We's only doin' you a good turn," said the nine-year-old newsy.

"It's all right. I was only tryin' to see if you would stop me. I'll cut it all out. I will never smoke again."

That boy did not have to be watched. He was good and kind to his little friends, and proved to be one of the best boys on the street. Two years later, when he graduated from the junior grade, in one of the ward schools, he came to the president, saying that his mother was poor and sickly and he had to go to work. He was sent to a wholesale house where was wanted a good honest boy.

The first question asked Mike was:

"Do you smoke cigarettes?" The president will never forget the manly, prompt reply. He was given a good position, and that boy today is traveling for a firm in

Cleveland, Ohio, at a big salary. The increased interest in the detail work taken by the boys themselves encouraged the president to believe that he was still on the right road to build these little street-boys up for good, not only for themselves but for doing good for others. Another case of interest in an unusual way of "doin' a good turn." A bright-eyed, red-faced boy, ten years old, came running into the president's office, one evening, almost out of breath, and after clearing the way through a long room, he stood before the officer, eyes sparkling with interest. He had something important to say. His elbows were bare, his pants torn, his cap merely a piece of cloth, with a rim strong enough to hold it in place. His name was Bluster, receiving it from the boys on account of his blustering manner of doing things.

"Say, pres.," yelled Bluster. "I want authority to lick a kid."

That was a strange request. While the president was thinking what to say he added.

"I must have permission fur de gang's after me. Dey're on me track." Not desiring the gang to enter the office and create a scene, consent was given for Bluster to use force, if necessary to defend himself. A smile of satisfaction came over Bluster's face. A smile that indicated that he had taken advantage of the president, and was now about to glory in it. After a moments thought he said.

"Say, pres., I already licked him."

"Who and what for?" was asked with considerable surprise.

"Fur swearin."

Before he could explain the details of the case, in rushed eight or ten boys, all talking at once. Bluster never smiled when the boys declared he wasn't an officer and had no business to "take the law into his own hands."

"That's all right," put in Bluster, "ain't we supposed to work fur each others good? Well, an' wasn't I 'tendin' to my own business on de corner. I wus standin' there crying all about de big fire, when a man frum de other side of the street calls fur me to come over. I starts an' so does Swipsey, I beats Swipsey, an' sells de man a paper, an' what does Swipsey do? Does he go about his business? No, he told the man to go to hell and used other swear words an' I saw our association wus receiving a black eye. It's no use to preach to Swipsey, de only way to bring him to his thinking is to lick him. He knows as well as youses that its agin de rules to swear. So I punched him. I turned him an' rolled him over until he cried enuf, an' promised he would not swear again. Then de gang came after me an' I runned to you."

The boys still declared he had no right to punish Swipsey without permission from the president. Quick as flash Bluster said:

"Say, pres., didn't I have permission?"

The president could do nothing but back Bluster up. He had given him full authority. At this juncture, Swipsey made his appearance. His hair disheveled, face and hands dirty, and clothes in a terrible condition. Swipsey listened to Bluster's story with a great deal of patience. He looked guilty.

"All we want to know," said the leader of the gang, "is whether we can punish a boy for violating the rules, even if we are not officers." That was a leading question, and experience had taught the president that it was a very wise thing to have any boy punish a member, and in his own way. The only provision made was that no badge must be taken away from a boy by a non-officer. Where a boy cannot be corrected by a fellow member, he must submit the case to an officer. This was agreed to and the boys were satisfied with the method used by Bluster. The two boys were made a little present, and they all left in their usual happy mood.

CHAPTER XIV.

The more experience the president had with the street-boys, boys who spent most of their time in selling papers or shining shoes, the greater his desire to keep in close personal touch with each boy. He had learned that it was not wise to censure a bad boy, to punish a boy who had violated any of the rules. That belonged entirely to the officers.

Some of the best suggestions for gaining the most good came from the boys, and boys whom the general public would ignore, pay no attention to. The boys were working out their own salvation. Solving the boy problem themselves.

The strongest argument for self-government, among boys, was solved by the boys, the sellers. This was when they began to bring to the president money and valuable articles they found on the streets, and the sincere, earnest request, in every case, "to please find the owner—it doesn't belong to me."

It was through the honesty of one of the hustling sellers that this new work was started, which became part of the great work and was carried on so successfully, and to such an extent that hundreds of valuable articles, from fifty cents in pennies to a diamond necklace, were found and returned to the owners. The following incident was the starting point.

A stranger gave a little seller, what he supposed was a new bright penny, for an evening paper, and passed on. The boy renewed his work, and a few moments later another gentleman purchased a paper, giving the boy a dime. In counting out nine cents, as change, the seller handed the man the new penny he had just received from a stranger. The customer said:

"My dear son, this is not a penny; it is a five dollar goldpiece."

"I didn't know it, sir", replied the boy. "If you will please to hold my papers I will run after the man and try to find him—this isn't mine."

Around the corner the lad went at full speed. Up and down the street he looked but failed to see his man. He returned very much disappointed.

"He's gone," he said, "here's your change—nine cents."

During this little talk a dozen or more newsboys gathered around the man and when they learned what had happened several of the boys said:

"Harry, what you goin' to do with the mon.?"

"Our president will tell us what to do, come on," replied the little merchant.

"President, I have already licked de kid."

See Page 42

Off the crowd started down the street, around the corner and a noisier lot of boys never entered the president's office.

Each of the twenty boys present wanted to explain what he knew about the transaction.

All the details of how the seller received the money, and how hard he had tried to find the real owner were gone over several times.

The president complimented not only the boy who received the gold, but the boys who were so deeply interested in trying to find the owner. An appreciative present was given to the boy, and it was understood that every effort possible would be made to find the owner. When it was first advertised a generous clothier, a lover of newsboys, presented the boy with a suit of clothes. After advertising thirty days and no owner claiming the five dollars, it was given to the boy. Nothing ever happened in the neighborhood where the newsboy lived that created such an excitement. The newsie posed as an honest boy, and was complimented by men and women, as well as being a hero among the boys and girls. Its effect was far-reaching, and did good not only to the boys, but it had a most desirable effect upon the people.

More particularly from this incident than any other did the newsboys "get next" and begin bringing to the president everything they found. Among the articles brought to him with instructions to find the owners, were diamonds, watches, money, in amounts ranging from fifty cents to eighty dollars; rings, robes, hats, gloves, valuable papers, badges of all kinds, handkerchiefs, money-saving banks, hundreds of addressed stamped letters, pictures, pocket-books of all kinds, keys, etc.

Among the live things the boys brought to the office was a dog. One afternoon, late in the autumn, four newsies walked into the president's office, talking and laughing, as they always do, and one of the boys, being "soaking wet," led a little woolly dog who seemed to enjoy the fun as well as the boys.

"My! how did you get so wet?" asked the president. "And what have we here?"

"A man trowed de dog into the river. He tried to drown him. I jumped into de water and saved him."

"Yes, president," said the hero, "I thought it would please you to save the dog's life."

Of course it pleased the president, and the boys agreed it was a very brave act. This little incident had its effect upon the boy, and they always looked upon him as a great fellow, and it wasn't long until they elected him to an important office.

It is a noticeable fact that newsboys have a peculiarly natural way of drawing, what they call, tramp dogs to them. Many a newsboy has been seen caring for a poor dog, who had either lost its owner or was hurt.

Sympathy is aroused very quickly. Often a poor, worthless dog has been taken into a seller's favorite lunch-room and given a square meal. From a boy who jumped into fifteen feet of water to save a little dog, something might be expected. He was watched. At one of the regular meetings of an auxiliary he showed the metal he was made of by introducing the following preamble and resolution, and spoke so strongly in its favor that it was passed unanimously.

> "WHEREAS, It has come to our notice that boys throughout the
> city, and boys, too, from our swell families, are killing the song

birds in the little patches of groves within the city limits, by the use of the Flobert rifle; therefore be it

Resolved, That the members of the Boyville Newsboys' Association bitterly disapprove of this wanton slaughter of our song birds, and we, therefore, pledge ourselves to do everything in our power to stop boys, whether members of this association or not, from killing, in any manner, these birds."

In his closing remarks he said: "If we expects people to show us kindness we must also do something what's right. And what can we do better'n protect the dumb animals. Let us show, what we are trying to get, kindness, justice and mercy."

A short time after the adoption of the above resolution one of the trustees attention was called to a member, a boy eleven years of age, who was very much worked up over the acts of some of his associates, not members of the association. The boys had made a trap and were trying to catch the robins that made their summer homes in the yards along the street.

The little boy always told his mother his troubles and in this case went to her for advice. She told him she would pray that God would tell the birds not to go near the trap. He seemed satisfied, but went away deeply buried in thought.

A few days later he was sitting on the fence, at his home, when the trustee passed. Knowing of the incident he asked the boy about the trap.

"Well, the trap was set all right," he said, "and my mother prayed hard, asking God to strengthen the instinct of the birds so they would keep out of danger—not go near the trap."

"Did God answer your mother's prayer?" asked the gentleman.

"Sure thing He did," the newsy quickly answered.

"Why were you so certain?"

"Because when it got dark I went to the barnyard and busted the trap all to pieces. There wasn't enough wood left to make a tooth pick."

The trustee slowly walked away saying to himself:

"Action was needed with prayer."

CHAPTER XV.

The individual interest in the monthly auxiliary meetings developed into schools of instructions. The boys began to learn how to debate, how to make a motion, to discuss any subject.

The vice-presidents of each auxiliary took personal interest in the details of the work, and kept the various committees busy.

The reports at each meeting showed how well the boys had the affairs of the association under control. In the meetings, the entertainment features were very interesting, from the fact that the boys themselves prepared the program. If it was necessary to secure talent, the executive committee required each boy, beginning with the officers, and then taking the names as the boys were registered in alphabetical order to show what he could do. First a boy, a bashful newsie, was required to "step forward and make a bow," and after several pretty rough introductions of this nature, it was always found that the victim began at once to prepare something for the next meeting. First, he would commit a very short piece, perhaps two lines, always selecting something of a comical nature. Then later, of his own composition. After a few efforts he became master of the platform, and was generally over anxious to do something.

It was surprising the different talents unearthed by this method. Musical turns, good, sweet singers, short and long recitations, original dialogues, and many "new stunts," as termed by the boys, when surprised at what someone produced.

The trustees always took advantage of this work, and did everything to encourage it. The talent thus discovered, and trained, in the auxiliaries, was used in the Sunday afternoon meetings to great advantage and honor to the boys.

At one of the Sunday meetings a very serious carrier asked the president: "How can a boy avoid being bad if he don't know what bad is?"

"How do you know bad money?" asked the president.

"I don't know bad money, I know good money."

A newsboy is never at a loss for a reply to any question, and knows something about any subject discussed in our daily papers. This boy further surprised the president by saying: "Those who are thoroughly skilled in navigation are as well acquainted with the coasts of the ocean, with the sands, the shallow places, and the rocks as the secure depths in the safest channels, and good boys must as well know the bad that they may avoid it as the good that they may embrace it."

Getting familiar with the headlines.

This boy occupied a front row for many months in all entertainments, and when a speaker interested him he paid very close attention. One time a very good minister was talking over the heads of the boys, preaching a sermon they could not understand. This little fellow, with his ever serious look, cried out:

"Say, mister, can't you cut some of that out?"

It had its effect, much to the embarrassment of the good divine.

It is one of the most difficult things in the oratorical world for any one to entertain newsboys. A speaker must not talk over them. He must become as a child and talk as a child, and he will be surprised to see what a good effect it has upon the boys. One time a very nervous boy, a seller from the avenue, became quite noisy and restless in the seat he generally occupied. The president observing this asked him if he would like a seat in the front row.

"Sure thing, I'll 'tend every Sunday if you give me this seat," pointing to a chair next to a post, where the president imagined he wanted to rest his head.

"It doesn't make any difference what boy occupies this seat," said the president to "Front Row Art," as he is called, "I want you to get the seat. I don't care what we are doing on the platform."

"Dis here is de dog."

See Page 46

One Sunday when the house was crowded to the doors, Art's seat was occupied by a boy about fourteen years of age, and much stronger than Art. While the speaker, a minister, was praying, the president saw Art at the door. He saw him push his way through the crowd and when at the platform, he took the boy, who occupied his chair, by the back of his neck and gave him such a shove along the seats that the young man was glad to reach the other end of the row. Art sat down, folded his arms, put his feet upon the platform, and eyed the speaker as if he had been there all the time.

Art was always ready with a smart answer to any question put to the boys. Even if his attention was directed to another part of the house, his little fingers were snapping, indicating his readiness to answer. His replies, while not always pertinent, gave the speaker a fair warning not to be too familiar in asking questions.

Art had a companion who was known as "Splinter," on account of his being rather slim, but no boy of his age, twelve years, ever had so many new movements as Splinter. He was never quiet, not so noisy, but continually annoying the boy who sat next to him. To take a companion's hat and throw it across the room, while some good minister was praying, was of frequent occurrence. He would answer questions without raising his hand, and would give the boy sitting next to him a knock of some kind before he stood up. With all this restlessness he was one of the best-hearted boys among the sellers. There was something in him that the president concluded he could not afford to lose sight of—just what that was did not develop enough to encourage.

At one of the Sunday meetings there was a speaker who knew how to hold the boys when asking questions. He had them perfectly quiet and recognized no answer unless the boy raised his hand.

He asked a question which required as an answer a verse in the Bible. To the president's embarrassment, "Splinter's" hand was high above the others and he kept a continual snapping of his fingers. He was determined to be recognized. The president was in hopes the speaker would pay no attention to him, fearing the reply would spoil the effect of the speaker's talk. However "Splinter" managed to be heard.

"That tall boy may answer," said the minister.

The sweat rolled down the president's forehead as he tried to get back into his chair.

"Splinter" arose, not a smile on his face. He looked serious, and without a quiver in his voice repeated, word for word, one of the longest verses in the Bible, and which gave an appropriate answer.

The speaker looked as surprised as the president, and the compliment he gave the boy was appreciated by all.

"Splinter's" education, after that, was looked after.

CHAPTER XVI.

An interesting case came to the president showing how one family can disgrace an entire neighborhood; can give a bad name to a whole street. On one of the small narrow streets within the two-mile circle, lived a family, man woman and five boys. One of the boys, a young man, served a term in the penitentiary for robbery. The names of two of them appeared on the police station blotter about three times a year for drunkenness. It was on account of these boys that the neighborhood gained such a bad reputation. The other two boys, John and Tom, ages nine and twelve, were newsboys. Boys who were driven from home, by the parents, "to get something to eat elsewhere." They frequently slept in stairways, old buildings, cellar-ways or any place where they could find shelter from the storms, or where they thought they would not be disturbed. These two newsboys were doing more to ruin boys on the street than the entire membership of the association, and when they came into the president's office seeking admission, the president concluded that if these boys could be saved, and their bad acts turned into good, Boyville would be a success. It wasn't necessary to ask them if they were eligible to membership, if they sold papers, if they were newsboys. Every word, every act told all that was required. With all the rags, and dirt, and slang talk, these boys were up-to-date in everything. All the leading topics of the day were discussed by them. Every base-ball player they knew by name, and it was discovered that all newsies followed them when they wanted to get into a ball-ground free, or into a circus. They had their own way, and without money. They feared nothing. They worked for themselves only. The little sympathy they had for any one was drowned in their eagerness to move on. They gave no thought for the morrow. There was no hesitancy by the officers in giving these boys membership cards, and when they received them, to the question, "Well, now boys, what does this mean?" they answered:

"We mean to lick any one as doesn't do right."

The vice-president, a smart young man with the courage of a lion, went to the boys' home to make an investigation of how they lived, and why they were so bad when on the streets. Here is what he discovered:

They lived in a small cottage and with a man and woman who were not their parents. Their own father had died leaving several valuable pieces of property to his wife, who was again married within a year, and to a man who soon lost all the property, having spent the money for liquor. The mother died, and her husband again married in less than a month, and to a woman who drank as much as he did. This was the home of the two newsboys.

"They both went to bed, nearly every night, with their clothes on," said the officer, "and what the boys had to eat wasn't fit for a dog."

The case was left entirely in the hands of the young officers with instructions to report within a month. In less than the appointed time a report was made. The two newsboys were brought into the president's office, each having on a nice suit of clothes, their faces and hands clean, and their general appearance and deportment remarkably improved.

"What did you do?" was asked the officer.

"We went to the house and demanded that the boys receive care and attention for what they were doing—they were bringing into the house from fifty to sixty cents a day earned by selling papers. And instead of the drunken man and woman spending this for whiskey, we made them buy good things to eat. A retail clothier gave us the suits of clothes, and the boys are simply good, and are working their way on the streets."

While the boys were working on this case the president reported to the humane officer the condition of things at this home, and in a very short time the family was quite respectable and the boys attending school. To the president, remarkable as seemed the turning of two bad boys into good, honest little sellers, the work of the two officers of the association with the parents was even more so.

Self-governing boys. Boys whom we think can do nothing, and seldom trust, for fear of failing, and yet they brought in line two of the worst cases Boyville had experienced.

As the weeks passed the two boys became favorites among their little friends.

One afternoon about six or eight months after the two boys became members, one of them, the younger, came running into the president's office, holding a roll of bills in his hand. Everybody had to get out of the way. He was followed by the "gang," some twenty boys, all looking at the little fellow with wonderment.

Roll of honor—some of the boys who turned in valuable articles
found on the street.

The Boyville Cadets—when first organized.

See Page 25

"See, here, pres., what I found," he said, laying fifteen dollars on the desk. "I found this at the post-office."

"And what do you want me to do with this?" asked the president. "I wants you to find the owner. That's what."

"Well, why didn't you blow it in? My! what a fortune you have."

"Blow it in? Would that be honest? No, sir, as soon as I found de dough I broughts it to you to tell us what we must do wid it, see?"

"That's all right," said the president, "and you are teaching us all a good lesson. How often we say; 'it is just like finding it.' and even grown people wish they could find money, and would they turn it over to someone, and ask him to please find the owner? Not that they would think they were doing anything wrong by keeping what they found; they simply never thought of trying to find the owner. You have done a great thing, and here is a bright, new dollar, for your honesty. I will advertise this in the daily papers for thirty days, and if I can't find the owner, it shall all go to you."

Proudly they walked out of the office, all trying to get closer to the happy finder, the honest boy.

The money was advertised, and in a few days the rightful owner was found. He wanted to see the newsboy. For his honesty he presented him with five dollars, adding: "In six months I want to see you in this hotel. In one year if you are reported all right by the officers of the association I want you to write me at this address." And he handed him his card, which gave Indianapolis, Indiana, as his home. Six months passed. The boy met him in the hotel. The officers reported that he was one of the finest and best boys on the street. A year passed, and one day he received a letter requesting him to "take the next train for Indianapolis, provided the president of Boyville says you do not swear, steal, lie or smoke cigarettes."

The president could truthfully vouch for all these, and the boy was sent to his new home. Seven years have passed, and that boy today is foreman of one of the largest manufacturing institutions in the state of Indiana.

What effect did the good work of these two boys have upon the family? It caused them to stand on the street posing as relatives to two honest boys.

Does it pay to take an interest in a bad boy?

A boy of eleven years of age made application to become a member. He was approved by the proper officers. A sealed note accompanied the application. It read: "He is accused of giving wrong change to customers, and runs away with money."

As soon as he received his membership card, and badge, and left the president's office two officers were on his track. They watched him sell papers. Three days passed when he "stumbled against something." A gentleman in the post-office gave him twenty-five cents for a morning paper. He had no change, but excused himself to "step across the way to get it." Instead of going into the store the little boy started in a run around the building and was lost from sight. The gentleman made this remark to a friend: "I might of expected it." This was overheard by two newsboys. One said: "Oh, no mister, your money is not lost. We'll have it for you in ten minutes. Don't you be uneasy. You stand right where you are for a few minutes."

Out ran the boys, one going to the right, the other to the left, and a third joined them who took to the alley. In less than ten minutes the boy was brought to bay, and appeared before the gentleman.

An apology was given, the money returned.

"Don't you say anything to him," said one of the newsboys, "we won't do a thing to him, oh, no." The man soon forgot the incident, and will never know the severe punishment that boy had to bear. They took him in the alley, bumped his head against the wall of the building, rolled him in the mud, took his badge from him and with a parting word of advice left him. The badge was turned over to the president with instructions to return it to the boy at the expiration of fifteen days. What for? The president did not know and only learned the particulars a month later from one of the officers. The boy called for his badge, and it was given to him without a word.

The books show that this same boy, after leaving the junior grade in school procured a good position and the proprietor particularly called attention to him for a peculiar trait. He said: "The boy applied for work, office work. We gave him a job. He asked particularly how many hours he must work. When he began and when he stopped. This given, we were surprised to see that he was at the office every morning two hours before his time, and pegging away at a typewriter. His wages have been increased three times. He'll be one of the firm before we're through with him.

"The only recommendation he had was that he was a member of The Boyville Newsboys' Association—and this we took. In fact, it proved a better recommendation than that offered by his mother, who called to get part of his wages to purchase whiskey."

PART FOURTH

Members of the East Side auxiliary.

CHAPTER XVII.

It was just before Christmas; the streets and stores were crowded with people purchasing presents.

An old lady was standing on the corner waiting for a street car. In her hand she held a small package, a Christmas present for someone. A boy, about fourteen years of age, darted out from a door-way, grabbed the package, hastened down the street and dodged into an alley. A newsboy who saw the act started after the thief, and as he ran several other newsboys joined in the chase. While they were gone another newsboy went to the lady expressing regret at her loss, but assuring her the boy who stole the package would be caught.

With tears in her eyes the old lady told the boy that the box contained a number of presents for a little girl who was confined to the house on account of being a cripple for life. That the purchase was the result of many weeks' hard work, sewing for some of her neighbors, that she might earn the money to get a present for the little girl.

"Now, my lady," said the newsboy, "don't you worry for a minute, one of our officers started in a dead run after him and I know he will catch him. We don't allow anything like that to happen. That boy don't belong to the association."

The lady was escorted to a drug store where people wait for cars, and advised to remain there until the newsboys returned. She did not have to wait long, for, in a short time, the officer returned with a dozen newsies all trying to push the "grafter" ahead of them. When in front of the lady, he was made to hand her the package, and get down upon his knees and ask her forgiveness. The old lady was placed upon a street-car, and the officers took charge of the boy. They brought him to the president's office.

"Mr. President," said a member of the executive committee, "we have here a new boy. He was pretending to sell papers on the streets, but he proved to be a 'grafter,' for we caught him stealing a package from an old lady who worked all summer to save money to buy a Christmas present for a little girl who is a cripple. We run him down." The boy hung his head. He was under no obligations to any of the boys, and could have been independant over his capture but when he was told the package belonged to a little cripple, it had a strange effect upon him. He lost sight of everything but the wrong done to the little girl.

"I didn't know it belonged to a cripple or I wouldn't have taken it. You see, we at home don't think nothing of taking things as we can get, we believe in helping ourselves to anything we wants when no body is looking. I am sorry I took the present."

The boy lived in a bad neighborhood. His father was dead, his mother had no influence over him, he roamed the streets at will, and spent the majority of his nights sleeping in freight-cars. He was just the kind of a boy who grows up along the docks of our lake cities, and takes advantage of every opportunity to steal anything he can use or care for without being detected, from freight depots or cars. This is the class of young men the association has been aiming to reach for a long time. The selling of papers being only a subterfuge for stealing. He was fifteen years old and admitted having done many bad things.

"It is boys like you," said the president, "who disgrace any association, and while no one seems to look after you, or want you, we will take you into the association and the officers will have you under their charge; what do you say to that?"

"Well, I guess you have me down pretty fine, and if I wants to ever get a job I must start my life over again."

"The boys will forget this little package act, and blot out all your bad deeds, if you will begin a new life, and I will guarantee that in six months, by the time warm weather comes, we will get you a nice position."

"If I would have known that package belonged to a little girl do you suppose I would have swiped it?" he added.

"It isn't that alone we object to. Every time you steal something someone suffers, and the only way to avoid injuring any one is not to steal at all," said the president.

"Aw! tell him to cut it out, cut it out, he kin do it just the same as we do," put in a little bootblack.

"Yes, but you don't have to go out on the street and takes what ever you kin carry home, like I do," he replied.

"Well, if your mother makes you do that we won't do a thing to her," said a seller, who claimed to own four corners.

The conversation ended by the president giving the new boy a membership card with instructions that he must report in thirty days.

Soon after he left the office, three members of the executive committee hastened to his home. The mother was warned that "this sending your boy out to steal must stop, and stop quick." They listened to no arguments, simply gave advice and orders, what must be done, and left.

A month passes and the day named for the new applicant to receive his badge, found him at the president's office, as is usual with boys, an hour before office hours.

"Gee, but I have lots of good friends. Some of the boys took me to see a show, some let me sell papers on their corners, but I had to cut out swearing."

The numbered badge was given him.

A member of the executive committee who had him in charge reported:

"He was hard to bring down to our way of doin' things. It was natural for him to steal as to eat, and he wanted to give the wrong change two or three times. We licked him three times. He was game. Give him his badge, he's all right."

Six months later this boy was given a position in a wholesale house. He began on the top floor to work his way up in the business.

His eagerness to learn, his willingness to do things not exactly as part of his duties caused his employers to notice him and he was advanced, in less than two years, to shipping clerk in one of the departments.

Here was a boy whose home life was degrading. His neighbors paying no attention to him or his family, except to say: "That boy ought to be turned over to the police." The newsboys, the boys we often look upon as being bad and useless, changed the life of this young man.

He is now slowly becoming one of the reliable business men of the future.

CHAPTER XVIII.

The president was about to board a street-car for home one evening, when a dozen newsboys came running towards him, calling him to "come here."

"Bundle found fifty-six dollars," was heard from a bunch of sellers. The president, of course had to return to his office.

Bundle was a little round, red-faced boy, who always wore a large scarf around his neck, and in most any kind of weather. The sellers were not surprised at any of their number finding money but, said a bootblack:

"What's going to happen when slow-pokey Bundle finds something?" But he did, and at the enterance of one of the largest buildings in the city.

"There it was," said Bundle, "all wide open before my eyes, I stumbled over it and the money scattered. Didn't it Sam?"

There was nothing in the roll to indicate its owner. Some one accustomed to carrying money in his vest pocket had lost it. As soon as Bundle picked it up, he called to the boys across the street and on the corners. A dozen boys answered him, and they all marched towards the president's office. Each boy had something to say.

"Say, pres., we come near losing you, didn't we?" said Bundle, "but if you did go home I would have stayed up all night holding the dough until you come to your office."

Bundle was rewarded, his companions were as delighted as he was. A happier lot of boys never walked the streets than these sellers.

The next morning, Bundle, with five other boys came into the office, their faces were long; Bundle looked sad.

"Bundle got a licking," said one of the boys looking sympathetically at Bundle. The president looked surprised.

"Got a licking, and what for?"

"His mother licked him because he brought the money to you. She said it belonged to her and she could spend it as she liked."

It was a fact that Bundle was severely punished.

"All the boys on the street saw me get a whipping," said Bundle, "and I don't like it."

The boys were assured that all would come out right in the end. "You just wait until we hear from the advertisement we put in the papers," said the president.

"Fire-top."

See Page 67

The boys were soon playing upon the street.

A prominent clothier saw the notice of the boy finding the money and his desire to seek the owner. He wrote the president: "If you will send that honest boy to me I will present him with the best suit of clothes in my store."

The mother accompanied Bundle to the store and not only did he receive a new suit of clothes but an overcoat as well.

Within forty-eight hours after the find was advertised the rightful owner appeared, received the money, and presented the boy with a five dollar bill and a good watch.

"Keep this watch to remind you that if you will follow up your honest beginning, you will not only be a rich man, but a good one."

The object of relating this incident is the sequel.

The big head-line compliments in the newspapers; the many little presents and congratulations Bundle received had a surprising effect upon his mother. She was proud of being the boy's mother. Her sons and daughters posed on the corners and pointed with pride to their brother.

Not only did this act have a good effect on the boy and the family, but upon the entire street, as the remark is often heard, "this is the street that has the honest newsboy."

CHAPTER XIX.

There are many interesting cases coming to the attention of persons interested in newsboys, and they all have a tendency to awaken sympathy.

Two little boys, ages nine and ten, were brought to the president one morning by an officer of the association. They were accused of fighting, "almost to a finish."

Between sobs and tears they both tried to tell why they were fighting. While telling their story, a boy about fourteen years of age entered the office. He was also crying, but more seriously. The president turned to him and sympathetically asked, "what is the matter?" With his hands rubbing his eyes he answered: "One of the newsies run out of the alley and throwed my papers into the gutter and they're all spoiled."

"Where did the boy go?"

"He runned away and left me alone."

"How many papers had you?"

"I had four."

The two boys that were crying, forgot their troubles and became interested in the other boy. Calling the two boys, the president asked them if they would run out and try to find the bad boy who threw the papers in the street. Of course they were delighted to go. Taking the crying fourteen-year-old newsboy by the hand, the little fellows left the office.

After waiting an hour, and no signs of the boys returning, the president went upon the street and to his surprise saw the two little boys, who were to hunt down the villain, playing together.

"Well, what was done with the boy who ruined Joe's stock of papers; did you find them?"

"You see, we went to the alley, we looked ebery place fur the kid as what threw de papers into de gutter, but he had skipped. So me an' Skinny talked it over quickly an' we just gave Joe eight cents an' told him to go home, to fade away, to forget it. As de case wus settled we thought it no use ter bother you wid dis trouble, an' we resumed our bizness."

Certainly a new way of settling troubles.

There is a small boy who has the reputation of being a little boss in the territory in which he sells, owing to his desire to settle all disputes in his own way. He goes upon the idea that it is absolutely necessary to resort to pretty severe punishment to gain a point.

One evening a boy about fifteen years of age came into the office, crying as a boy only can; the tears found considerable trouble in working their way down his cheeks, making his face look as if furrows were established for a time at least. On the left side of his forehead were several clear spots, round in shape, which he pointed to with considerable feeling. The president's sympathy was aroused, and to the question, how he was hurt, he replied:

"Firetop—licked—me. He—hit—me—with—his—fist."

Firetop was not over nine years of age, and the president knew of his fighting qualities, but somehow no one ever presented any charges worthy of investigation. His name, the boys said, "came to him on account of his red hair." His reputation for honesty was never questioned. He was simply a fighter. He was one of the most successful sellers on the street. Because he was a "pusher, he went every place, and asked every person he met to buy a paper." While the boy was telling his story, three other members dropped into the office. They stood for sometime looking at the poor boy.

"Do you boys know Firetop?" asked the president.

"Certainly, we all know him."

"Well, you go out and try to find him and tell him I want him to come here immediately."

Out the boys went and when on the sidewalk started in different directions to find Firetop. Ten minutes passed when Firetop came running into the office. The boys had found him but he was too fleet of foot for them.

"Pres., they tell me you wants me, what fur?"

"Look at that boy's face," said the president, pointing to the injured lad who began to cry in earnest.

"I see it. I did it. But say, kid" turning to the boy, "what did I do it fur. Look up at me; say, what did I do it fur?"

"For nothin'," came a faint reply.

"Come off, I hain't going 'round doin' things fur nothin'. Answer me, you kin talk, what did I do it fur?"

No reply.

"Didn't I punch you fur swearing at a lady?"

It was some moments before the boy answered, and he drawled out, "yes."

Firetop then told the story. The boy was selling papers on the street, he asked a lady to buy a paper, and because she refused he swore at her, using language seldom seen in print.

"I heard it, an' I told him it was against the rules, an' if he didn't cut it out I would punk him. What did he do but swore at me. He violated the rules before my face. I punked, gently at first, an' then I punked him again. He ran into the alley, I followed him, an' de boys come from the street, I told them he was my game, an' I punked him again. I told all the boys I would punk de gang ef they came to help him. Say, pres., wasn't I right in punking him?" The boy acknowledged he swore and Firetop kept at him until he promised he would never do it again. This was accomplished with very little trouble. The boy's face was washed and as there was no traces of a wound the matter was amicably settled. The boys left the office, good friends.

CHAPTER XX.

This incident recalls another case of swearing, and the peculiar method adopted to correct a boy, as well as to influence a family to train their son in the right path. One reason why so many boys swear is because they constantly hear men swear on the streets. At Sunday-school the boy learns that he is violating one of the commandments. But men pay no attention to it, then why should boys? Boys are imitative. They want to do what men do. It is seldom that we hear of a mother approving of her boy swearing and encouraging him in this, certainly vulgar habit. This method used by the president in curing a boy of swearing, may not meet the approval of many of our Sunday-school teachers, and it is given with some reluctance. It is given, however, to show what can be done in extreme cases.

"Are you the president of the Newsboys' association?" asked a boy with a very pretty face.

"Yes, and what can I do for you?"

"I want to join the association."

The usual questions were asked and answered. He proved to be a carrier and had twenty-eight customers. A membership card was given the boy with instructions to call in thirty days and get the badge.

The boy left the office perfectly happy. In about a week he returned, walked to the desk and laid his membership card down, saying: "My mother says I can swear all I want to, and you have nothing to do with it. You must not tell me to stop swearing."

The president turned around, looked at the boy for a moment, discovered he was unusually bright, and back behind his black eyes he showed the right kind of spirit indicating that if he made up his mind to do a thing he would do it.

"So your mother wants you to swear. Well, well, and she don't want you to belong to any association unless we all swear. Well, you shall not be made unhappy. If your mother wants you to swear you shall have that pleasure. Does she swear?"

"Yes, sir, we all swear to beat the band," he replied, and in a tone indicating that it was one of the pleasures of his home life.

"And don't any of you think it wrong to swear?"

"Oh, no, father says he can swear and it gives force to his arguments. Mother says if I want to swear I can do it."

"He sweared at a lady and I punked him."

See Page 67

"This association compels no one to stop swearing—the rule adopted by the boys simply says we don't believe in it. And the officers wouldn't for the world have you do anything to displease your parents.

"How many swear words do you know?"

He thought for a moment counting on his fingers, then said:

"I know seven."

"Seven big swear words, well, well, and can you name them to me?"

"Yes, sir, all of them and I may know another."

"All right. Try it. One, two, three, four, five, six; my! that's an awful bad one, and—and—seven. There they are."

In repeating the words, his manner showed he was familiar with their use. Not a blush rose to his cheeks.

"Do you want to be a member of this association?"

"Yes, sir, all my friends are members and they want me to join."

"I will pin your card before me, on the desk. See?"

"Yes, sir, I see it."

"Well, I will let it remain there until you call for it, either to tell me to tear it up or you take it. Now, here is what I want you to do. And this not unless you want to. You go home, and every time your mother wants you to do something use one of those seven swear words, and say it loud enough so she can hear it. Keep this up until she tells you to stop that swearing."

"I will do it, but suppose she licks me, then what?"

"Oh, that would hardly be in keeping with her teachings, she wants you to swear, doesn't she?"

"Sure thing, she never licks me for swearing."

"Do you want to stop it and become a member of the association? Well, you try this plan, and if you can, throw the entire lot at her, the seven words, all at once."

"Well, I'll try it. It looks easy."

The boy left the office with a hearty "goodby."

The following Saturday he returned. He stood smiling at the desk.

"You can give me the membership card," he said laughing.

Recognizing him the president shook him by the hand.

"Well, I have been wondering what luck you had in swearing."

"Oh, I had luck. Only got licked seven times."

"Got licked, and by whom?"

"Well, you would think the whole house fell on top of me. Father said, send that boy down to you at once, but mother licked me until I saw stars. I'll never swear again in our home. She stopped it. She said she never heard such terrible swearing and when I said I learned it of her, I got the seventh licking. Gee, but I was sore for a week. Mother told me the first thing this morning to come after that card."

"What did you do when you first went home?"

"Oh, I threw those seven swear words right at her, and, from the very beginning. She looked at me several times. I backed up, and when she asked me a question, I let fly the worst word, then I had to run."

"What did your father say?"

"He only said, 'didn't I tell you that some day that boy would disgrace us, now it's up to you to straighten it out,' and when they knew I told you why the card was sent back, that changed everything. I've been down here four times, father made me go."

His name was placed upon the books, a badge was given him, "with a lucky number," and he left the office.

A month later the president met him at one of the auxiliary meetings, and to the question, "How about the seven swear words," he said:

"We busted up swearing at our house. Everybody had to stop it."

No better worker on the street can be found than this boy. His whole soul is in the work for doing good among his associates.

PART FIFTH

Carriers.

Carriers.

CHAPTER XXI.

There is no subject that has received so much attention and has worried so many good people as the liquor question. Saloons and drinking never cease to be problems for our well-meaning temperance people. Why man created saloons, no one undertakes to answer. The strongest man is never too strong in a saloon, and the weak is to be pitied. The saloon is an evil that has been with us a long time and seems to be here to stay in one form or another. While we cannot eradicate the evil, especially by extreme methods, can we not modify its influence? We have tried the probation method, and failed. We have tried the open saloon, the clubs, the no-treating, the open reform saloon, the wet and dry division—but the saloons are still with us, and this because of the fact that the state, the city, property owners, recognize the saloon legally, through the assessment of heavy licenses and taxes, and good well-meaning people ask and receive money from the ever-willing giver, the saloonman, and use it for charitable as well as church purposes. The world today is heartless in its mad rush for money getting, and the "graft" is in the minds of thousands of well-meaning, but over-anxious to get-rich-quick men; among them the saloonman. Let us suggest to our saloonmen how they can stop a great deal of misery in the world. We have in mind a saloon that was "made good" by five newsboys. "A real live saloon, where politicians congregated to lay plans for work, and whose owner had an eye to making money, and saw nothing else, even to the ruining of boys and men."

"Say, pres.," said a newsboy from the saloon district, and an officer of an auxiliary, "Jimmy Smith is drunk and laying in the alley at the saloon where politicians hold their meetin's. The bar-tender throwed him out."

The books showed Jimmy Smith's father was a "ward politician," a good fellow who was often taken home drunk by his son, a newsboy. Jimmy was eleven years old, very bright and intelligent for his age. He learned to drink liquor through his father and mother sending him to the saloon for beer, and "dropping in the alley on the way home and tasting the beer, until he began to like it."

To the question, "did you ever see Jimmy drink in the saloon?" the boys answered that it was a common thing; "but today when the bar-tender took Jimmy's nickel, and he was full, he throwed him out. He said he didn't want the kid to disgrace his place."

Three of the best officers were called, they went to the alley, and took Jimmy home. Three of the five boys who were assigned this case, belonged to a gang and were familiar with all the inside workings of a saloon, they were never slow in showing their appreciation of a saloonman who defended them, and who turned them down for entering the saloon. The method adopted by the boys was their work. They knew the proprietor of the saloon, and knew him to be a very kind-hearted man. No person ever asked him in vain for a donation to any cause. His own boys were model young men, stood high in school, and associated with the best of church members. Strange to say the two sons of the saloonman were regular at Sunday-school. It is a fact that when any society, church or other organization desired aid, this saloonman was sought after by a dozen persons. They knew he was easy. This man in his home, on the street, in the lodge room (and he belonged to many societies), in any public gathering, was recognized as an honest man; but behind the bar he saw nothing but money.

He never thought he was doing a wrong by taking the last cent from a drunken man; it was business, and that was why he was there. When reminded of it he simply replied that, "I might as well have it as any one else, for someone will get it." Often he said: "He is bound to drink and the best way is to let him drink up all his money and that is an end of it."

When the newsboys called upon him to plead for their friend, Jimmy, they were received with, "the utmost attention and kindness." The following is what the chairman reported:

"We said to the boss, we come to see you about Jimmy Smith and his father. You see Jimmy has been in bad company, the bad company was at his home, his father an' mother. He learned the habit of drinking by tasting beer he was sent after by his father, and he said when he learned to drink that your clerk gave him a glass of beer every time he came after it. So the other day your bar-tender threw him out of the saloon. He had gradually taught the boy to drink, and when he began to get so that it annoyed him, he didn't want him. We come to see if you won't please stop giving Jimmy any more drink and tell your man to throw him out of the saloon before he drinks. We'll stand for that, but we won't stand for his pitching him in the alley when he's got all of Jimmy's money and is drunk. As to his father, we don't want you to sell him anything when you see he has enough. Don't take the last cent he has when you know he is full already. Send him home. His family needs every cent. And don't sell Jimmy any beer if he comes with the bucket."

The boys were treated with great kindness by the owner of the saloon who promised to do more than they asked of him. His bar-tenders were instructed, under penalty of dismissal, not to permit a newsboy in the saloon.

"I realize the wrong being done to the boys," he said to the president, "and it is through thoughtlessness that we permit the boys to come here at all. I'll tell you what I'll do. One of my relatives has an interest in a commercial college. I'll buy this boy, Jimmy, a scholarship if he'll go to school."

Jimmy was only too glad to accept.

Two years pass, and Jimmy is about to graduate from the college. The manager said: "I have four men after this boy. He has the right kind of push in him to make a splendid business man."

Four years later Jimmy received a monthly salary of $100, and during that time has assisted in helping many a street boy.

CHAPTER XXII.

At one of the auxiliary meetings the vice-president of the association, who was always practical in his talks to the boys, gave a little advice to the sellers.

It is worth remembering.

"Boys," he said, "rain or shine be at your post, at your corner. Never be out of papers, and never be out of change. Many a good boy who needs money loses a sale for want of having change. Keep your eye peeled. If a man wants a paper, you should see it, though he is a square away. I know of one little boy, smaller than those who were selling with him, who always saw a customer a block away, and when the evening's work was over he generally had ten to twenty cents to the clear more than others. Be polite and always cheerful. Keep your face and hands clean, and you will get many an extra nickel. If you are polite and civil you will get a regular line of customers who will always wait for you. Thank everyone who buys a paper. Tip your hat to the ladies and they will speak well of you when they get home. Any little favor you can do for a man or woman on the street (and not look as though you expect something), will always bring you business. The wind blew off the hat of a gentleman one day, and a little seller saw it. Quick as a flash he ran after it, took his own cap to wipe the dirt off the gentleman's hat, and handed it to him. The gentleman said: 'How many papers you got?' 'Twenty-four, sir,' said the boy. 'Give them all to me.'"

On the membership card it reads: "He does not approve of swearing, etc."

A probation member, a boy who received his membership card, and had thirty days to wait for his badge, brought an old member to the president, one evening, with this plea.

"President, this boy swears like hell. I heard him on the corner."

"Aw, what you given us, you swear yourself." replied the accused.

"Yes that's all right. Tell me something; how would I know what swearing was if I didn't know something about it," proudly answered the new member.

"Well, you have no right to bring me here and accuse me of doing what you yourself do. Read your card, kid, read your card."

First sale of the day.

Without showing any signs of worry, the little fellow said.

"President what can you expect of a bationist. When I get my badge things will be different. I cuts swearing out then."

"Yes, but you better wait instead of buttin in before you are a live member," said the carrier.

They talked some time about the matter between themselves and finally they locked arms, slowly walked out of the office saying:

"Guess we better cut out swearing all around."

The following story illustrates a good method of treating boys who disobey their parents. It may not meet the approval of many fathers and mothers, but the sequel has in it the success of the work among the street-boys. We regret that we cannot give due credit to the author for the suggestions embodied in the story.

A young boy was left alone in the yard to play. Everybody had gone and left the house in his care. He was given the key and told not to enter the house until the family returned. After a while he became tired of the birds, the flowers, the the trees, the sunshine. The spirit of disobedience entered into him and slowly he took his way to the house. He unlocked the door. The first thing met his eye was his father's razor. He had always been forbidden to touch it. But the spirit of license ran riot in his veins, and in using it he cut his face until the blood trickled down. Next he made his way to a matchbox. He had always been told to let it alone. He first built fences with matches on the floor, then fires under the lace curtains. A hole in the carpet, ruined curtains and his fingers blistered was the result. Suffering with pain and ashamed of his disobedience he steals out under the trees, and like Adam in the garden, he thought he could hide his sins by hiding himself. So he stole away and crawled under some bushes. When his father came home, discovered the ruined articles, he thought, what can be done to restore and mend that which his boy had broken, had ruined? His razor was broken, but he could buy a new one. His matches were consumed, but he could buy more. The curtains and carpet were defaced by fire, but they could be replaced and repaired. Wealth could repair the damage done to the house and make all as before. Skill and nature could repair the wrong done to the hand and the face, and make them as they were before.

But where were the riches and where was the teacher that could make the boy's heart as it was before his disobedience? None could be found. Let me tell you what happened. The father came not to upbraid, but to entreat; not to chastise, but to weep; The child's hand was burned, the father's heart was broken. The boy cried for shame, the father cried for sorrow. The father put his arms about the boy and with his head upon his breast together they sobbed out their sorrow. One part of it was the boy's confession, and the other part of it was the father's pain. Together they made a new resolution and hand to hand, and heart to heart, and love to love, they began together to repair the ruin that had been wrought.

During the early stages of a boy's membership he is constantly reminded that some day he will leave the street, he will seek employment elsewhere, and his start in a business life depends upon his street work. To illustrate this teaching, a boy found a small child's savings bank. It was filled with money, small coin; and it was heavy. It was picked up on the street over a mile from the president's office. As soon as found, the boy started on a run, as they always do, for the office. It was delivered with the usual instruction "to please find the owner." To try the newsie the president called him aside and said, in a confidential whisper: "Why didn't you sneak around the corner, into an alley, any place where no one could see you, and take a stone break the old bank all to pieces, take the money, and, my, what a good time you could have had."

The boy quickly replied: "No, sir, Mr. President, suppose I wanted a job, and stood in line to be questioned by the man, and he would ask, have you always been honest? What would I say? Why! my face would show I did something wrong—I took a little bank from some poor boy, and he would say, I don't want a boy I would have to be afraid of; no that don't belong to me."

This plainly shows what can be successfully impressed upon the minds of these hustling, seemingly thoughtless, street-boys. And when the owner of that bank proved to be a little girl—and how happy she was when it was found and returned to her, the boy said: "I would rather have the girl's smiles than all the money the bank contained."

PART SIXTH

CHAPTER XXIII.

From the very beginning of the Boyville association there has scarcely been a day without something of importance transpiring among the boys. It has been gradually building up, incidents and noble acts showing the willingness of these boys not only to do right themselves but to assist others.

The work so humbly begun in 1892, with one hundred or more members, mostly the poorest boys of the streets, little outcasts, as they are often called, developed so rapidly under the self-governing plan, that in the early part of the year 1905 the books of the Boyville Newsboys' Association showed a membership of over three thousand boys under fourteen years of age. This enrollment includes two hundred and fifty boys who started with the association as sellers and shiners of shoes, but who today have graduated from the street. The majority of this number are engaged in some business, lawyers, doctors, commercial travelers, clerks or working in some trade, and all ambitious not only to earn a living for themselves but also to lend a helping hand to those who are in need, ever having in mind the teachings of the association. The following will show how well some of the principles have been remembered and how long they remained intact.

Early in January of 1905, a young man brought to the president an old pocket-book containing twenty-two dollars and sixty cents ($22.60), together with some letters, the contents of which revealed the fact that the owner was a poor woman and had been visiting her relatives to secure assistance in raising money to pay taxes, long since due, on her home. Names were given, but no residence.

The president said to the young man: "You know we advertise what the boys find in the daily papers and do everything we can to seek the owner and—"

"Yes, sir," replied the young man, "I know all this and have been through it many years ago. That is just what I want you to do, please try to find the rightful owner. I want no compensation, and I don't want my name mentioned in any way."

As it was necessary to know who the finder was, so that after the expiration of thirty days the money could be returned to him, he finally gave his name and address. When he had left the office, something about his eyes reminded the president that he had seen him, somewhere many years ago. Bringing out the Newsboys' book he found among the first names recorded eleven years ago, this young man's. Following the name was: "Seller, and shiner, age eleven, poor parents, smart boy," and on leaving the street, as a seller, became a graduate member. So, he was a newsboy eleven years ago, and still retained the desire to do something for others.

Lining up ready to go to church.

About a week after the money was advertised, a very aged lady called. She minutely described the contents of the pocket-book; she said: "I was returning from a visit to my son, where I went to get $22.60 to pay taxes on my home. This amount included some back taxes. The property was already advertised for sale. What to do when I lost that money I did not know. My mental suffering was most intense. I walked from the depot towards the court house and did not miss my pocket-book until I crossed the bridge. Yes, this is mine."

During the recital of her story her eyes were filled with tears, and she showed the mental strain under which she was laboring. When the pocket-book and the money were handed to her, the change in her demeanor was beautiful to behold. When the young man was told to whom the money belonged and the great good it did, he said:

"No money reward could pay me for this. I am only too glad we found the owner, especially as it belonged to so poor a woman."

Does it pay to be a life-member of The Boyville Newsboys' Association?

CHAPTER XXIV.

The finding of valuable articles and turning them over to the president, with a request to find the owner, is not a rule of the association.

All these little acts have a tendency to cultivate a desire to assist others and many times violations of the rules are corrected by members who are not officers.

At almost any time of the day can be seen a man with a two-wheeled cart, slowly circulating around newspaper offices, especially about the time the dailies are out. The newsies purchase a penny's worth of ice cream, or cheap candies, and often these old men become quite confidential friends of certain boys—particularly the shiners, who are on the street almost constantly. One time a new member, a bootblack, a boy about fourteen years of age, before he understood the secret workings of the association, had a dispute with a vendor of ice cream and peanuts, about the loss of several sacks of peanuts. The boy was accused of stealing the peanuts. "Yes, you didn't see me steal 'em," said the shiner, "an if you don't catch a feller, how youse goin' to prove it?"

The boy was about to leave the wagon, when several sellers came to him.

"Say, Muddy Water," cried one of the boys, "we seed you steal the peanuts. You must settle wid de ole man."

The boy came back, but pleaded that he did not have any money.

"All right, we'll chip in an' pay de debt."

The money was raised, and the boy was required to pay for the stolen peanuts and make an apology.

"I'm sorry, but I didn't know it was again' the rules of the association," he said.

"Of course it's again the rules, an' it's our business to give all new members warning when they do things like that. Don't do it any more."

This was a warning well heeded as after events proved.

One of the greatest benefits gained by the newsboys in belonging to the association is the securing of suitable positions; for boys, as they grow older, naturally leave the street work.

Wholesale as well as retail men, frequently ask for good, honest boys. During the twelve years existence of Boyville it has been the delight of the president to secure some two hundred places for newsboys. With all this great number it is a pleasure to state that not one in fifty proved unworthy of the positions, or unfitted for the kind of work. The majority of boys for whom positions were secured were from very poor parents, mostly widowed mothers, needing their assistance.

Unless a person is familiar with street boys, no conception can be formed of their energy and determination in following up anything they want.

A young man, who had outgrown newsboy's work called upon the president and wanted a position as brakeman on one of the railroads.

He was kindly informed by the president that he knew the superintendent of the road he wished to work for had already over five hundred applications from young men wanting to be brakemen. Instead of asking the president to see the superintendent, as is generally done, he said:

"Please give me the name of the man who does the employing of brakemen. I want to see him. I think I can show him he wants me."

"I am afraid it won't be of any use, but I like your pluck. Here is a note to him."

This note simply said the bearer was an honest young man.

A few days later the young man called.

"Well, I got a job. I'm brakeman on one of the fast trains."

This he secured through his own tact, for this certainly was necessary. His street experience taught him to hustle for himself, and it became part of his nature as he grew older. He did not sit down and wait for something to come his way, for something to turn up. He turned up something for himself.

His frank and honorable method of working the superintendent, his earnest but manly appeal, his push, his politeness, his tact, secured for him what five hundred young men were "waiting to receive by letter." When the matter was referred to the superintendent he said: "His every action showed he was a willing worker and not afraid to work overtime if necessary. He works as though he owned the entire road."

CHAPTER XXV.

Commercial men, some of our best merchants, sometimes, in their eagerness to make money, forget the first principles of honesty, and often make assertions that upon second thought they would not make. Sometimes in their advertising they will say things which they would never think of saying under other circumstances, though lying in business matters is equally as dishonorable as in private life. The relations between the public and the merchant, as well as between master and servant, must rest on mutual respect and confidence. Here is an illustration, by a close observer, a boy fourteen years of age.

Walking along one of the principal streets, a newsboy noticed the following sign, in large type, in a show window and attached to some article for sale. It read: "Regular price, one hundred dollars. Our price, twenty-nine dollars."

"Say, president," said the boy, "is that man telling the truth when he says a twenty-nine dollar article is worth one hundred dollars?"

It was a question that required a wise answer, but put it in any business way possible, nothing could satisfy the boy that it was strictly honest.

"When I go into business," said the seller, "you bet I'll not fool the public; when I say a thing is worth so much it will be worth that much."

What time would develop, what changes come over this young man, no one could tell, but the right principle had a good hold of the boy, and it meant success and a clear conscience during his manhood.

That the success of the association does not depend upon the efforts of the officers entirely, will be seen by the following:

Three newsboys called upon the president; two of them were leading a ragged little fellow with a shining-box thrown over his shoulder.

"Say, president," said one of them, "here's a boy shining shoes on the market an' the way he swears is puttin' men out o' business."

The accused bootblack was a sight. To the question where he lived he replied: "I have no home. My father's dead an' my mother, she's no good. There's no room fur me in the house."

By further questioning it was learned that the clothes he had on were given to him some two months ago and had not been taken off since he put them on. This may seem strange, but it is only one of the dozen of cases where parents do not require the removal of their boy's clothes when they go to bed.

The tough from market space.

See Page 89

The peculiar odor coming from boys who are treated in this shameful manner will prove this. This boy walked from a neighboring city, or stole a ride on some freight-train. He had been shining shoes around the market-space for a month or more, and declared that to be in the push, to be recognized by men, and to secure business, it was necessary to swear and be tough.

"I wouldn't be a bootblack," he said, "if I couldn't swear, the men wouldn't shine if I didn't."

The newsboys who frequented the market were very much put out by this boy's swearing and general tough appearance, so when opportunity favored they began their missionary work, with the result of persuading the shiner to accompany them to the president's office.

The boy had a very attractive face. He was worth saving.

"So, you come to see me about joining the association," said the president.

The boy replied: "The boys say I can make more money if I cut out swearin' an' belong to the association."

"They tell me you swear and sometimes don't know how to give correct change to your customers. If that's so you are just the kind of a boy we want. You little hustling fellows make our best young men. You don't wait until someone comes to you for a shine. I have seen you follow a man who had red shoes a whole square. You will make a good business man, and these little boys, friends of yours, are just the kind of boys who will help you, will bring you business, will tell you where to get something good to eat, and I think we can throw away your old ragged clothes and get a new suit, how would you like that?"

His face had a surprised look. He didn't expect some one to offer anything of interest to him, he expected to get lectured, to be "talked goodygood to," as he afterwards said.

"Well, you see, mister," said the boy with some familiarity, "we can't do business on the street unless we do as men do. They swear at us an' we must swear at them or we lose the shine."

"How often do men swear at you?"

"How often? I can't count 'em. Every other word."

"Well, it doesn't sound nice, does it?"

"No, an' I could cut it out."

"Sure thing he can cut it out, an' we'll be right behind to see that he forgets it," put in one of the newsies.

"Well, I'll start you in the association," said the president, "but I don't want you to be too good to start with. Sometimes you may forget what the card means, and you will swear before you know it, but don't let that worry you, the next time you will do better and forget it. But when you get the badge, in thirty days, then you mustn't swear at all, for if you do the officers will be right after you and your name will be on a list that means something when you get older and want a position in some big store."

The membership card was given to him, a new suit of clothes was furnished by a kind hearted clothier, and the boys—including the chairman of the executive committee—took the boy home. When his mother discovered some one took an interest in him, she began to think he amounted to something, and from that time on, he received attention. At the expiration of thirty days the numbered badge was given to him and he started on his new life.

In the fall of the same year this bootblack was unanimously elected as an officer of Boyville, and is one of the best boys on the street. Two months later he brought to the president a gold watch, worth forty-two dollars and fifty cents. The owner was found, and insisted upon seeing the young man. He was sent, with the watch, to him. The wealthy lawyer handed him ten cents, and gave him some good advice. The boy returned the money saying:

"No, Mister, you keep this, you need it more than I do."

CHAPTER XXVI.

Among the great number of boys who called at the office, none cast such a ray of sunshine about him as a little seller known as Sunny Willie, on account of the smile he always seemed to have. But with all his good nature and kindness of heart, he, at times, became very serious.

One evening after the boys had sold their papers and were enroute to their homes, Sunny Willie, as was often his habit, called upon the president to say good night. Just as he was leaving the office, two boys walked in and the loud talking between them indicated trouble. Willie concluded to remain. Leaning against the desk he became a very attentive listener. The smile had left him. He looked thoughtful.

"I know you're wrong," said one of the boys, "you're talking to hear yourself talk. You are looking fur trouble. That's what you are. I ken prove it. I ken show you I wasn't on the corner fur a week." "That's right," replied the other boy, "why wasn't you there fur a week, because you stole the papers from the poor old woman and was ashamed to sell 'round the corner. Now, come off, you took de papers."

At the corner of the post-office is a small stand kept by a woman, who has been engaged in selling papers for a number of years. One morning, some papers were missing from a bundle lying upon the sidewalk. The boy accused usually sold papers on the corner and his absence for several mornings gave rise to the suspicion that he either took the papers or knew something about them.

"As I said before," continued the accused boy, "I did not steal the papers, an' you got no proof to show I did."

There was silence for some moments when Sunny Willie, said, in a whisper, to the president:

"I saw de kid take the papers. Shall I butt in?"

"Yes, you arbitrate the case—settle it," replied the president.

The usual smile was still missing when Willie said, quietly:

"Sand the track, you're slipping."

"What do you mean?" asked the boy, his face becoming very red.

"You know the rule of the association is to warn a boy when he's slipping; when he's doin' something wrong. When I say, sand the track, I mean you can't go forward, you go backward, and some one must help you or you slide back, see? I'm the fellow who's ready to stop you from sliding. I saw you take the papers."

The accused was surprised. He could not talk. Sunny Willie again came to his rescue.

"I'll give you these pennies," he said, and the smile returned to his pretty face. In his little hand he held ten new pennies.

"Now, didn't you take the papers?"

"Yes, but I intended to return the money for them, or make it all right with the old woman."

"Come," he continued addressing Willie, "I'll go with you and we'll make it all right."

Out the three boys went and they were soon talking with the old woman. Shortly, Sunny Willie returned to the office.

"If I hadn't a put sand on his track he would have slipped way back," he said to the president, "Everything's all right. He will never steal papers again."

Another little seller, a favorite on the street among business men, one of whom the president often purchases a paper to please the newsboy, came running into the office one evening and throwing his bundle upon the lap of the president said:

"Here, pres., hold these papers until I go into the hotel to get a drink of water."

The act was done so quickly the president found the big bundle on his lap before he really understood the wishes of the newsie, but he quickly returned, took the papers, and said, as he hastened out:

"Thank you, Mr. President."

The confidence this boy had in the president was appreciated, not only by him but by those who witnessed the act.

It has always been a source of great pleasure, to the president and his associates, to see how deeply interested the officers of the association become, as the following will show.

Three officers were walking on one of the principal streets casually looking in the show-windows when they heard music; looking ahead they saw a newsboy, a seller, walking along, playing a mouth-organ. Coming to him, it was noticed the instrument was an unusually fine one, and a new one.

"That mouth-organ is too expensive for that boy, there's something wrong," said one of the officers.

"Where did you get that organ," was asked the newsie.

"I bought it at Smith's store, down yonder," was the reply.

"Well, I guess, not. You never had so much money. Come on with us and show us where you bought it."

They walked to the corner when the boy said:

"I didn't buy it there, I bought it down on Monroe street," giving the correct name of a store on that street.

Dividing the papers.

"All, right, come along, we'll go down there."

Around the corner they started and when within a block of the street the boy again changed the place of purchase.

"I buyed it of Mr. Jones, way out on this street."

That was five blocks away.

"Now this is the last time," said one of the officers, "if you change the place again, look out."

But when they had walked four squares the boy again made an effort to change.

"No, you don't my chappy," said one of the officers, "We know you stole it. We knew it from the first. Now you own to the truth or we will take you to the president, and then what?"

The boy squirmed considerable, but every movement gave evidence that he stole it.

"Now, where did you get it?" was bluntly asked, as the boy was backed up against a building.

This was too much for him. He owned he "hooked it." Naming a prominent department store as the place he took it.

"You must go with us, hand it to the proprietor and beg his pardon," said the officers.

This at first seemed a most difficult task, but when they promised to accompany him to the store he agreed.

When at the door of the great store he asked the officers to step aside.

"If I do this you will not tell the president, will you?"

"Of course not, he shall never know anything about it."

He walked in, took an elevator and soon stood before the manager of the store.

He told how he saw it on the counter and "hooked it when the girls were not looking, but I will never do anything like this again."

The manager thanked the boy for his determination to do better and told him he would forgive him for the theft, and promised to give him a position in the store if the officers of the association would bring him there when he was through school.

The president learned of this incident a month later but never knew the name of the newsboy.

CHAPTER XXVII.

As has been said, the boys are continually suggesting by their acts and words, something new, something whereby the officers can build upon their ideas.

The membership cards were given first, to show the boys some of the written rules; and, second, that the boys might have something official to show in case they lost their badges; but a new idea suggested itself to one of the graduating sellers, who was about to engage in business other than selling papers. A prominent churchman advertised, "a boy wanted in his manufacturing concern." This young man saw the advertisement and became an applicant for the position. He was received very kindly and naturally so because he had an honest face, and was a willing worker. The gentleman asked if the boy could give any reference.

The newsboy took from his pocket a membership card of the Boyville Newsboys' Association.

"Do you know any thing about the association of newsboys?" asked the seller.

"Yes, sir, I know all about them."

"This is my reference," the boy replied handing him the card on which the man read—"He does not approve of swearing, stealing, lying etc."

To the boy's surprise and disgust, the gentleman took the card crumpled it in his hand, and threw it upon the floor, remarking: "that's no reference—that's no good in business."

The boy picked it up, and, to use his own language, said:

"I waited until my temper cooled down and I asked him, 'can you say you never swore, never stole any thing, never gambled, never cheated any one? I can, sir, and that's what that card means. I wouldn't work for you.' Oh, I hit him hard. As I was leaving he called me back, but I said, 'if you would give me five thousand dollars a year I wouldn't work for you. You have not only insulted me but the association.'"

CHAPTER XXVIII.

Before Boyville was thought of, a personal investigation into the home-life of over a hundred boys was made, and this covered a period of three years. Of the one hundred who were graduating from the street work as newsboys not more than thirty were engaged in a business that would lead them to fortune or fame. Seventy were satisfied with making a living by earnings of vice and petty crimes. It was learned that a boy who was permitted to go on in his own way would have no useful training for later work. The seventy boys followed the rule of men in wrong-doing. "No man is guilty until caught," is the general rule of men who make it a business of stealing.

The progress of any humanitarian legislation is gradual.

No one ever stopped to make inquiry about a newsboy. He lived in a business, and social circle, all by himself. He was left to shift for himself and in a most unequal battle.

When investigation revealed the deplorable fact that seventy per cent. of our newsboys were being educated and trained with their faces towards jails and penitentiaries, the question arose, how can we reduce this number, how can we turn their faces towards a better life, a happier condition, a delightful ending? How make them honorable citizens, good men, loved by all who know them, an honor to themselves, to their parents, their friends, the State and city in which they live?

The problem solved itself in personal experiences, convincing us that we must try to catch the candidates for prison before they have been debased and to keep them decent. "It is the Christian, decent, brotherly way for one thing, and it is the cheapest way in dollars and cents for another."

It is a rule, rather than an exception, that people have always considered a newsboy bad, and he is therefore treated accordingly.

Everybody knows or can soon learn to know, that the street is the great school of crime. Betting and gambling are typical of the combination of work and play of man and boy that street work produces.

One of the greatest evils of the street was that of begging; of boys working on the sympathies of the public by taking advantage of men and women on street-cars or in public places.

Some boys made a business of begging, the majority not from their own choice, but by compulsion of their parents.

One boy in particular was doing more to injure the success of the association's work on the street than hundreds of others who were bad in other lines.

The father of this boy would wait until the theatres were out, at night, and instruct the boy to "work the car," by begging, and if that failed by forcing papers upon young men who were compelled to purchase what they did not want.

It took some time, almost a year, to stop this kind of business, and then the president had to call upon the efficient Humane officer to stop it. As every case of begging was traced to the fault of parents the Humane Society had to deal directly with them.

The Boyville association gradually stamped this evil entirely out.

Two new members.

To stop begging, stealing, swearing and gambling, four leading street evils among the newsboys and in guiding the footsteps of these little wanderers, for this they are when seen upon the streets of our great cities, that Boyville came into existence, and it is to co-operate, when it is possible or desirable, with the parents and the home in reclaiming boys who have gone astray or are likely to follow paths that lead to ruin.

There is no greater, stronger sign of love to young or old than when a friend gives a warning in the right spirit.

The children of Israel had no better friend than Moses, and when they obeyed his warning they never went astray. We may be wrong in our liberal methods of giving to charity; we may be wrong in dropping pennies into the hats of the street beggars—the blind—the lame—the crippled who stand or sit on our public streets pleading in a tone of experience; and we may be satisfying an ever-warning conscience; but there is one thing certain, we can never make a mistake by warning a newsboy from doing anything wrong—from stealing, lying, swearing, or gambling, and it is always wise and safe to give a boy the right start in life.

In every city, with a population of one hundred thousand or more, thirty per cent. of the newsboys, the sellers, have no homes or their homes are worse than none at all. If men and women would stop to think, to investigate, listen to the stories as told by these street boys; of the wants, miseries and degradation in the sad conditions that surround many of them; these dirty, ragged boys would receive a more Christian-like attention and care. If your nature to mingle with the meek and lowly is forced, if your mission for doing good in this world is cast in other fields, where better results may be reached, you can take a personal interest in seeing that those who are familiar with work among street boys, and who delight in trying to aid them, are given proper encouragement and assistance so that their work may be carried on successfully.

CHAPTER XXIX.

A few months' experience with boys who spend most of their lives upon the street, and pride themselves on being tough, will teach one a great lesson. You will learn you cannot reach a boy unless you get near him, are of his kind; and the most lasting and truest friendship, and through which you can gain the best results, is where you place a boy under personal obligations to you, through kindness. You may buy him for money, but he does not look upon you with the same interest and confidence as when you gain his love through personal attention. The boy must be understood. No two boys are alike. Though many are endowed with similar characteristics, each has his own individuality. The trees are not all of one kind. Even the leaves on the same tree differ in size and contour. One tree in the writer's yard, one of the choicest of plums; a long branch sprouted out every spring and grew so rapidly that before the leaves in the fall began to show signs of decay, it became strong and reached several feet beyond any other branch. It made the tree look awkward, unnatural, but when trimmed down, even with the others, it produced more and better fruit than any other portion of the tree. The boys are like the birds who are unlike in plumage and song; the flowers in color and fragrance, and yet nature would not be perfect were it not for these different lines of beauty, strength, and fragrance.

In the cultivation of plants the gardner considers the nature and needs of different stages of growth, furnishing the nourishment and care that will be most helpful just at that time. So in boyhood we observe various stages of development, whose natures and needs must be studied that we may properly provide for them.

It has been said: "That the home, the church, the school with their natural and uplifting influences have been responsible in the past, and must continue to be in the future, for the manhood and womanhood of this nation." It is a well-known fact that the home sometimes fails, or there is no home, or one which the church and the school do not reach. There are times when even these have no power over a boy's acts. A boy who violates the laws of the land is answerable not to the home, the church or the school, but to the State.

Crime among boys, in America, is greatly on the increase. The reports, official and unofficial, that are made public, of the per cent. of the criminals serving time in our jails, workhouses, reform schools, and even our penitentiaries, are astounding, and almost beyond belief.

How to check this is a problem of the greatest importance, and it cannot be solved without the hearty co-operation of every person.

Among the first things to be done must be the recognition of the power of home and our neighbors. We cannot live without our neighbor. Each home depends upon some other home; and when the boy leaves his home to go upon the street, he is at once overcome by the stronger power and influence of a boy of some other home, and, perhaps where the rearing and training was not good. The boy is a result more or less, of all influences and environment of the lives of his companions. Every good mother recalls the pang that came over her heart when for the first time she led her boy to school, knowing that her influence must be shared with that of the teacher. It is not long until the boy quotes his teacher, and sometimes in defiance, when he says: "My teacher says so an' so." And how many times we hear this from the boy when away from home, more frequently than the sayings of his mother. The boy's school life soon begins to develop self-reliance, full of possibilities, of curiosity and questionings, the period of formation of thoughts, feelings and desires. And when a boy reaches that stage in his life when he is permitted to go down town alone—he at once begins a new life. And there is not a mother in our country but who makes this pleading request to her son as he is about to start: "Don't go into bad company."

It is on this line that the Newsboys' Association, with all its varied interests and objects, through its many channels of work, backed with that true spirit of Christianity characteristic of everything that means good, with the aid of its president and its many working officers, in the name of God and humanity, aims to make the bad boy of the streets of our cities and towns good, so that the mother will not find it necessary to say: "Now, my dear son, don't go into bad company."

Let us all hope, and pray, and work for the time to come when there will be no "bad company" on the streets.

CHAPTER XXX.

At one of the auxiliary meetings the question was asked a carrier, why the association "kicked against drinking whiskey when my father drinks four times a day." In a talk at the meeting the vice-president said: "Your father may have been a respected citizen. He was all right when he started out, but today he is a physical wreck, I know him. He drinks too much. He paid no attention to warning. Perhaps he had no one to tell him. He trembles now, and I have seen him fall to the ground, helpless. Some day he will fall and get up no more. Every boy has in his mind a real desire to do good, but if you start in life as a whiskey drinker, if you stand around and see your friends drink without giving them a warning, some day you will regret it, something will come up in your life to remind you of your carelessness, your lost opportunity to help a fellow being, and his ruin means more to you than you think it does.

"There was a man once rowing in a small boat above Niagara Falls, where the water was quiet. He got funny and ventured down stream too far until he got into the current and not having strength enough to pull out of it, he was going faster and every second he saw certain destruction ahead of him. It was too late for him to think and act. The thinking should have been done up the river on peaceful waters. So you boys better do your thinking now if you don't want to follow that kind of people over the brink. No, boys, don't drink intoxicating liquors, don't start it, cut it out, forget it.

"We do not believe that temperance is really promoted by compulsion, but this we do know, that the boy who will let whiskey and all spirits alone is very fortunate, and has a bright, happy future. He is the boy who will succeed; he is the young man that is wanted; he will be the man to be trusted."

"Tenements on the avenue."
In these old buildings, at one time, lived seventeen families.

See Page 105

CHAPTER XXXI.

The problem of the boy is a great one, and the more we have to do with his life upon the street the greater the task of solution becomes. It is said that two great factors make the sum of human life—heredity and environment. We are told that if you will gather up soil from the arctic regions and carry it on a steamer southward, you will soon see it covered with vegetation. If the soil of the tropics is taken to the frozen regions of Franz Joseph Land, it will become barren. The soil of both regions is full of heredity, but the difference of environment greatly modifies the result. There are in all of us hereditary tendencies to both vice and virtue, and under favorable surroundings, these tendencies will be either dormant or developed.

A thief may come from a morally healthy family, a happy prosperous home, but he is an unhealthy exception not the rule. It is the offense of our day that the tendency of life is toward destruction of character. The crowding of population to the cities, is gradually destroying the home feeling. This rapidly increasing rush from the country and small towns to the centres of individual energy, brings a dependent class of boys, and the official reports show a significant increase in the number of juvenile criminals, from small towns, and also that they are much younger than formerly. This does not mean that the energetic young man of the country should stay away from the cities, or should not seek employment or business in a city; it simply means that christian people should take a greater personal interest in trying to make the boy good before he leaves his home, and that the city people should make city life purer.

So long as our best reputed citizens, the first men of many of our churches, own the dilapidated tenement houses, receiving from such occupants a rental sufficient to pay taxes, and without caring who occupies the premises or for what purposes, the criminal tendency must increase.

For a time charitably-inclined people may check and partially correct an evil, but the tendency will remain, sure to assert itself in one form or another. If the present cheap-John tenements should be wiped out, and it were made possible for the proper classes to secure homes in the country, modest as necessarily they would be, it would go a long way towards correcting one of the greatest evils of the day.

"The prison returns of one of our great States show that fifty per cent. of all young criminals come from bad homes, from tenement houses owned by rich men, and only nine per cent. from good homes."

Since the Humane societies are so well organized, and doing such magnificent work, much may be expected for the better in the condition of the houses of the poor. There are many streets in our great cities where people shudder when compelled to walk, on account of their bad reputation.

The tenants may be bad, but are they worse than the owners of the property? Have you ever stopped to think who owns a building under whose roof lives a dozen bad characters?

One Sunday morning, a gentleman in the city was walking down an avenue of considerable importance when he was surprised to see two young newsboys coming out of the rear door of a saloon, each trying to keep the other from falling to the ground.

The building was old and rickety. On the second floor were not a half dozen whole panes of glass in eight window frames.

Astonished at this, a question was asked, of a passer-by who owned the saloon property?

"Mr. — — owns all the property on that side of the street. He is now teaching a Sunday-school class while boys are in his building drinking. This thing's repeated every Sunday. It's headquarters for young men."

When our leading men of business, our wealthy citizens, men of influence, men who stand high in the commercial world, are renting their property to persons who, for the money they make, are ruining hundreds of young lives, what can we expect?

We need an era of enforcement of law, less of pretense, more of purpose. Whether the laws be good or bad, is not a question. If they are good, they should be enforced for the welfare of the community and the vindication of the State. If they are bad, they should be enforced so that their injustice may prove sufficiently oppressive to lead to their appeal.

The saloons will always be with us, and so long as the State, and the city receive the price for their existence, and grant them recognition and endorsement, they should be protected in accordance with the laws governing their business, but beyond all this, there is a law, a moral law, a law of decency, of respect, for the welfare and happiness of mankind, that should appeal to every man engaged in the selling of liquors.

Five men, of our acquaintance, engaged in the saloon business, have for many years mutually agreed to do certain things. They do not open their places of business on Sunday. They do not admit a minor into their saloons for any cause. They will not sell liquor to a man who shows the least sign of being intoxicated.

If every man engaged in the saloon business would follow to the letter these few simple rules, thousands of good wives, and innocent children would be happy, and the influence for good could not be estimated. Our Sunday-closing laws should be enforced.

The lives of a majority of men, hard-working men, are dreary enough for six days of the week without having all of the desolation compressed into the seventh and drilled into them through the avarice of selfish men who aim to take advantage of a man under the influence of liquor, and take from him his last cent and then throw him into the street.

We are learning to regard the majority of youthful offenders, especially in our large cities, as the victims of environment, sufferers from lack of opportunity for good. In nine cases out of ten, boys who are found in saloons come from well-to-do families, and are permitted to be there through neglect and carelessness of their parents.

CHAPTER XXXII.

A question is often asked, why young men do not more frequently attend church services. May not one of these reasons be traced to neglect and carelessness on the part of the parents? Nothing in the religious world can be more important than the proper training of young men. It is said that the only place where real religion can be taught is in the home. By this it is not meant religious forms, but real religion. To go to church every Sunday and sing religious hymns and listen to eloquent sermons is not all there is to religion. The formation of character, the stimulus of the moral sentiments must be done largely outside of the doors of the church. To assist in building up the boy who roams our streets at will, and to take an interest in and to encourage the boy to live up to and follow the instructions he receives at his home, is, indeed, to practice real religion.

"I will buy from the little fellow."

It is a well-known fact, often repeated by the guards at our penitentiaries, that no man ever entered these institutions but what at sometime or other declared that, if he had followed the admonition and religious instructions of his father and mother, his life would have been different. If father and mother do not practice in their daily lives this real religion, and if the boy is not brought up to believe that some people are to be avoided, and held in contempt, all the churches in the world cannot correct such mistakes, because they have but few hours one day in a week to accomplish what six days can undo.

It will be seen, then, how important it is that the boy on the street, whether he comes from a good religious home or a bad home, should be watched and carefully guided and taught.

Our work in the garden is not to pull out onions, radishes, tomato plants, but carefully to destroy the weeds, and not only those weeds that are crowding the tender plants, but all weeds. Get the wild sprouts out, pull up the weeds by the roots and throw them away. This a good gardener will do, and he will carefully pull the soft, rich earth around the plants to brace them up.

Waiting for the last edition.

If the same interest is taken in our newsboys, to pull out the weeds so that the boy can grow, it will be doing what the preacher often says: "A good man's goodness lies not hid in himself alone; but when he endeavors to strengthen his weaker brother."

CHAPTER XXXIII.

Men often lose great opportunities to assist their fellow-men through neglect, through carelessness and indifference. It is so easy to say, "you have my sympathy, you are doing a noble work," when many times the speaker may be better adapted for the same kind of work and be far more successful. And so an opportunity is allowed to slip by all for the lack of taking advantage of it.

The influence a man or a woman teacher has over a boy is wonderful. In the eyes of a boy, a teacher stands for a model of perfection and is supposed to be in reality, in daily life and actions, what he seems to be when he shows his best side to the pupils.

From the school, from the teacher, from a trusted friend, the boy carries the influence back to the family, into his daily life upon the streets, and many of the teachings follow him through life. The boy at school is taught to be kind, to be generous, and to remember his little friends whenever opportunity favors. Heartfelt sympathy in a newsboy, comes like a flash of lightning, and he is ever ready to fall in line when the boys want to remember a friend. The president was taken by surprise one day when the street sellers, the poorest of our newsboys, through one of their hustlers, presented him with a gold badge. The money to purchase it was raised by subscriptions from the boys, in amounts ranging from two cents to twenty-five. A few days after the presentation the president was walking on one of the main streets when he was accosted by a little seller, from the opposite side of the street.

"Say, president, come over here."

A boy never called the president to go where he wanted him to go but he complied at once, and cheerfully. The little ragged fellow stepped in front of him and said:

"Pres., have youse got de gold badge we gives you?"

"Yes, here it is," and the badge was taken from the coat and handed to the boy. Looking at it closely, and calling several companions to him, he said:

"Pres., youse see that diamond in the center?" pointing a dirty finger to it.

"Yes, sir, we all see it, and it's a beauty."

"Well, you see," he said straightening up above his natural height, "I subscribed four cents to this here badge, and all the boys put up the dough. When I went home and thought it over, I says to myself, we ought to have a bigger badge than this fur our president. So when I comes down town I see de boys and we concluded to have a diamond put in the center. It met wid de kids 'proval, and it was done. You see de diamond?"

"Yes," replied a dozen voices.

"Well, I blowed eleven cents in it," he proudly replied. Adding, "Ain't it a bird?"

Happy youth.

CHAPTER XXXIV.

How many prayers have been offered for the salvation of the slums; how many sighs and expressions of regret and sympathy have been given, by well-meaning people, for the "poor and unhealthy boys of the slums."

Those who are familiar, and it is to be regretted that they are so few, with the real conditions of these, supposed, unhealthy and certainly unpleasant districts, will substantiate the declaration that the boys who live there, in these ill-favored spots, and who have followed the vocation of selling papers or shining shoes, until they arrived at that age when it was necessary to seek other and more lucrative employment, are ninety per cent. healthier and stronger and better able to fight disease than boys raised in the most sanitary districts and in wealthy families. The slums of Whitechapel and Westminster, in London, inhabitated by a squalid and criminal population, as well as the slums in New York and other American cities, maintain a healthier condition among the inhabitants.

In a period of six years, with an enrollment of two hundred and fifty news-boys, who belonged to the sellers auxiliary; a majority of them living in what is called "the worst part of the city, the most unhealthy; the most degraded; the most undesirable," and boys who from necessity were compelled to sell papers or shine shoes, thus requiring an almost daily appearance upon the streets in all kinds of weather, there were but three cases of sickness, and but one death, and this death was caused by an explosion at a Fourth of July celebration.

Little Barney Frank, one of the brightest and most promising members of the association died January 28, 1903, having been injured by a toy cannon.

The president attended the funeral of this little boy and being asked to say something touching the life of his friend, he said:

"Barney was an exceptionally bright and happy boy, loved by his companions, and almost worshiped by his heart-broken parents. His happy disposition, his smiles and great interest in his fellow newsboys will live forever in the hearts of those who knew him. It is often asked why are the young and innocent taken from us? Some of us believe that the road to heaven opens wide to welcome little boys.

"One of the most pleasing remembrances of Barney's life was shown in the following incident. It was a cold November evening, with a heavy fall of rain and sleet. I was standing in the street looking for a car to take me home, when little Barney came running to me and said: 'You go in the store, in a dry place, I'll watch for the car and I'll call you,' and in spite of protestations, he stood in the rain until the car passed. So it was always with Barney, ever looking after the happiness of his friends."

They took the remains to another town, and buried him in a village graveyard. There he rests in peace. In summer the grass grows green and the daisies and violets keep watch; and in a tree, whose branches shade the unmarked grave, there comes a robin red-breast, and every morning at the rising of the sun, and every evening just as the sun is sinking behind the hills, he sings his song of love.

Who knows but that it is an angel who comes to the grave of that little newsboy?

**"Billy Butcher, we must have an understandin',
which corner ob de street will you take?"**

PART SEVENTH

CHAPTER XXXV.

After more than fifteen years' experience among the newsboys we can say with considerable force, that the only way to give substantial assistance to the poor boy is to give him a start in life, helping him to work his own way through a hundred little temptations that would easily lead him wrong. Today Boyville Association boasts that it has driven from the streets of a great city all kinds of begging, gambling, swearing, smoking cigarettes, and instead of insulting, impudent newsboys, we have the finest lot of gentlemanly young business men in the world.

How to carry on successfully work of this kind, with results as previously stated, is the desire and wish of thousands of people in our country today. A person must bring himself in touch with the boy, he must learn his ways, his habits, by so doing he learns the best way to approach him and gain his confidence. This done, the rest is easy, because the boy works with you and you simply guide.

Education cannot be given, it must be achieved, and the value of an education lies not only in the possession, but also in the struggle to secure it.

Everybody knows that the infallible receipt for happiness, is to do good, and under the right conditions it is as natural for character to become beautiful as for a flower. In scores of instances it has been seen that the principles early established in the minds of the street-boys, especially where they are watched by their companions, and warned when they do something wrong, leave a lasting impression that time cannot efface.

Life is full of opportunities for the young man to do good, and if in his early career he begins to do right it soon becomes part of his life. The street-boys who first join the association are so gradually led into the good fellowship of their own making that the toughest natures thaw out, they are subjugated, submit cheerfully to the controlling powers of truth and honesty. Their manners soften, their words become more gentle and their actions show a willingness to be little gentlemen. The good that is in them is brought out by their own unselfish acts, and the hidden sleeping humanity bursts into a fuller life.

Today it takes a high order of men to succeed.

With the world as a competitor, where profits are figured by fractions, it requires young men of brains, combined with hard common sense, men of good moral characters, and a willingness to work.

For a young man to reach a rich inheritance he must work; he must remember that the root qualities of character are sobriety, industry, unselfish economy, and he must be honest in all that the word implies. Swearing, stealing, grafting inclinations, expecting something for nothing, smoking cigarettes or drinking intoxicating liquors will prevent securing good positions.

Already some of our great railroad systems will not employ a young man who drinks intoxicating liquors, or smokes cigarettes; and some go so far as to forbid swearing while on duty.

To gain this rich inheritance, to build up the boy who has no chance in life, who, in many cities, is regarded as a sort of a pest, something to be kicked and cuffed out of the way, is the great aim of the Boyville Newsboys' Association. It is a kindergarten in the great school of business and citizenship, and many years experience proves conclusively not only that the boy of the street is capable of conquering himself, and of mastering his own will-power, but also that he can assist his companions, to be honest, patriotic, and self-reliant.

Many a boy goes astray simply because home lacks sunshine. If home is the place where faces are sour and words harsh, and the boy is continually hampered with don'ts and censures, he will spend as many hours as possible elsewhere. A personal investigation of twenty homes of boys who were upon the streets a greater portion of their time, especially at meal hours or after nine o'clock at night, revealed the fact that nine boys were away from their homes on account of there being no restriction on the part of the parents. These nine families did not know, did not care, at what hour their sons returned at night, or whether they were at home at meal hours or not.

Home should keep in sympathy with a boy. His little troubles, his sorrows are made much easier and lighter through attention and sympathy, and if the boy can't get this at home he will go elsewhere; and he will often find it in society he would otherwise shun. No boy ever grows too old for love. And should the boy seek companionship in our crowded streets and discover some one in whom he can place confidence, his whole life is wrapped up in that love.

CHAPTER XXXVI.

In the Boyville Association it has always been the rule that, no matter how great a wrong committed by a boy, and the fine or sentence be what it may, if the boy looks forward to doing better, to putting his whole soul into trying to do right, if he hates and despises the act committed, that boy has a right to be honorably reinstated, and is heartily welcomed back to his friends.

"Often" says a thoughtful writer, "men and women mourn over past wrong-doings with which their present identity has no connection."

A good preacher once asked a despondent soul, whose life was shadowed by a wrong committed in early years: "Would you do the same thing again?"

"Do it again?" answered the man, "No, a thousand times, no."

"Then," said the preacher, "You have outgrown the conditions that caused the wrong-doing, and you are no longer responsible for it."

The best way to correct wrong-doing is to prevent it, to warn a boy against the evil vices that tend to his ruin in later years. And one way to prevent crime is to reward virtue.

Hon. Ben. B. Lindsey, of Denver, Colorado, Judge of the County and Juvenile Court of Denver, after many years of hard work, intermingled with the kind of experience that brings good results, declares that in the work of the Juvenile Court he has found a way to make our boys of today, who are inclined to be bad, follow paths of virtue and honesty that will lead them to good and honorable citizenship, and his success has been along the same self-governing plan of the Boyville Association.

We do not think there has been a more interesting official report nor one of so great a value to the thinking people as the publication of "The Problem of the Children and How the State of Colorado Cares for them," by Hon. Ben. B. Lindsey.

"Power under any law," writes Judge Lindsey, "may be abused. Mistakes under any law may be made. No system is perfect. If any conceives the idea that the Juvenile Court was created for the purpose of correcting or reforming every disorderly child, they are, of course, mistaken. Jails and criminal courts never did that. On the contrary, criminality among the youth of this country has been amazingly on the increase. Over half of the inmates of jails, reformatories and prisons combined are under twenty-four years of age. They are there largely because of uncorrected delinquency in childhood. While the Juvenile Court and probation system will not, and cannot, entirely overcome delinquency and waywardness, it will do a great deal better than the jail and criminal court ever did. The Juvenile

Court generally deals with cases in which there has been a failure in the home, the school, and often the church. These three institutions are the places through their various influences to form the character of the child. The Juvenile Court is rather an aid to the home and the school in the moral training of the child. If these two latter fail, the court, through its officers, can supply the deficiency. In the Denver Juvenile Court none are convicted of crime or subjected to the contamination of the jail.

"He was fishing in the lake."

See Page 120

"The Juvenile Court does not tolerate the idea of the child being a criminal. It does not consider the question of punishment the important thing. If the child cannot be corrected at home, for its own good and for the good of society at large, it is simply sent to a State public school, where discipline is superior to that of the home, and where it is intended to correct waywardness and to serve as an example to prevent waywardness in others. The purpose is, in delinquent cases, to inspire and receive obedience, to improve and strengthen character. We never release a boy upon probation until he is impressed with the idea that he must obey. It is explained what the consequences will be if he does not obey and keep his word. It is kindly, but firmly impressed why all this is so, and why, after all, he is the one we are most interested in and that it is for him we are working and not against him. We want him to work with us and not against us. He must, to do this, obey in the home, in the school, and of course, he must obey the laws of the land and respect the rights of others. We must know that he obeys. We know this by reports from the school, signed by the teacher, every two weeks; by reports from the neighborhood, when necessary to investigate, and frequently, by reports from the home, and, in exceptional cases, visits to the home. And more important than all this is the trust and confidence we impose upon the boy himself through the administrative work of the Court. We arouse his sense of responsibility. We understand him as best we can, and we make him understand us as best we can."

Nothing could be said or written of the history of Boyville and the intention of its workers that could explain the great object in view better than the above report.

CHAPTER XXXVII.

There is a city ordinance in Chicago which prohibits fishing in the lakes of the city parks, and persons caught doing so are treated as trespassers. No one would blame a boy for wanting to fish.

A boy, ten years old, left home with line and hook for one of these artificial lakes. After securing a pole from the drift-wood near-by, he sought an inviting spot to fish; and amid the green bushes, the songs of the birds and the breeze that brought sunshine to his young heart, he cast his line into the peaceful uninhabitated waters.

A protector of the peace, a defender of the law, saw this little boy fishing in public waters. While earnestly waiting for a bite the boy was arrested. He was taken, by the policeman, to the station. He did not have any friends to give bond for him, so they locked him up and left him there all night in a cell alongside of men who were in there swearing and cursing, using the vilest of language. He was placed with hardened people whose association could not be anything but injurious to a ten-year-old boy. Next day he was brought into Police Court, accused of fishing in the lake, sentenced for violating this great and important law of the city of Chicago, and sent to the work-house, to serve a time in the city prison.

This was twenty years ago, and, just such incidents as this, caused good honest-thinking people to try to introduce something that would protect and care for similar cases. Now, the boy who violates a law is not arrested and placed in jail or even a Police Station, but under the splendid Juvenile Court system the boy is brought into the presence of a judge who has an opportunity of showing what he would like to do in other courts, by extending an encouraging hand to the wayfaring boy.

The boy is greeted kindly and the strange feeling, which even men and women have under similar circumstances, is removed. Instead of the judge looking sternly at the criminal, as has been too often the custom, thinking, perhaps justly, the dignity of the law requires it, he kindly explains to the boy where he has made a mistake, where he has violated some law; and after gaining the friendship and confidence of the little offender, he is placed in charge of a kind-hearted Probation Officer, who personally looks after the interests and welfare of the accused. The Juvenile Court has power to require the boy to go to school, and the boy is impressed with the fact that it is for his benefit. Truant boys are looked after by this method, and the Probation Officer goes so far as to visit the homes of the boys to learn their surroundings. This has been the means of influencing many families to take better care of their homes and to keep things in a neat and tidy condition. This has never been accomplished before by any methods of a legal nature.

With the valuable work of the Juvenile Court and the Humane societies, together with the self-governing plan of the Newsboys associations, all working harmoniously, what must naturally be expected of the boy? The home is the natural environment in which to develop a boy in the direction of true, self-sustaining manhood; and it should furnish the conditions most likely to bring about the happiest results, not only to the individual and the family, but also to the State. When this fails, as it often does, the Juvenile Court steps in and the results are wonderful.

CHAPTER XXXVIII.

Boyville has made itself known to all classes of citizens, and has attracted intelligent attention throughout the country. The newsboys have learned to work together harmoniously, and this is one of the valuable secrets of human society that all must learn in order to be successful and happy. In the auxiliary monthly meetings the newsboys conduct the business with more decorum and intelligence than the average political conventions. So much for the self-governing plan.

The following interesting talk on "The Evils of Cigarette Smoking" was part of an address delivered at one of the Sunday afternoon meetings, and is well worth the time spent in reading:

"Smoking cigarettes causes both insanity and the degeneracy that ends in crime. The cigarette slave is always enfeebled in body, in mind, or in moral sense, and generally in all three. Whatever be the cause—whether it is opium and other drugs mixed with tobacco, or oil created in the paper by burning, or the immediate absorption of the nicotine from the lungs by the blood, to be lodged in every nerve and brain-cell in the system—the fact remains beyond dispute that the cigarette is a deadly poison.

"It not only deprives the blood of the proper quantity of oxygen and thus prevents its purification, but it also loads it with filth, so that the heart becomes clogged and the delicate convolutions of the brain, upon which the mind's attitude toward intellectual concepts and moral principles depends, are paralyzed. Cigarette smoking also creates a perpetual irritation, like unquenchable thirst, in the nervous system. It sets up a continual discomfort, a kind of a gnawing in the nerves, which makes the victim eternally uneasy except while he is inhaling the poison into his lungs. The result of all this is, that he lives in a constant state of nervous excitement, which reacts upon his poisoned brain and makes him incapable of serious and consecutive thought. His body is weary all the time, except when it is being stimulated by the alcohol which cigarette slaves inevitably seek and find, and at last cannot do without. It is a fact that crime and cigarettes nearly always go together. Prison records show that criminals, almost without exception, are cigarette slaves. Such is the history of the cigarette slave, and while, if he is a natural man of good family history, education, intelligence and ample means, he may avoid crime, yet he is in eternal danger. Boys, newsboys, for your own interest and welfare, for the love you have for your parents, if you are cigarette smokers, stop it at once. If not—do not begin."

Pastime—the beginning.

CHAPTER XXXIX.

The question is often asked: "Do you want us to go out upon the streets and bring those ragged, dirty boys with us into our churches, and have them sit in the same pew with us?"

No, indeed, no. Both you and the boys would be unhappy.

The idea is for you to take an interest in preparing them for your church. To shove them out of your way, into the gutter, and say, "they are only newsboys," will never bring these boys to you or into your churches. They are the strayed sheep.

When upon the street you meet these "dirty brats," instead of avoiding them, of paying no attention to them, say pleasantly, "Good morning," and say it in a tone that means you are sincere and really wish them a very good morning. That would be easy and a thousand times better than to throw them money, as you, perhaps, have often done, to get rid of them, or thinking you have done them a great act of charity. All this costs you nothing.

Instead of having in your heart the desire to destroy; encourage the desire to rescue, to uplift. Instead of hating, cultivate love. "Go forth into the world and seek for light and light is yours."

If you would learn the secret of real happiness, mingle with the children. They are messengers which come to bless.

But you must understand them. They will teach you things you never knew or dreamed of.

A speaker at one of the auxiliary meetings asked a boy to give him an illustration of, "who is my neighbor?"

He answered: "This morning I shoveled off the snow from the sidewalks in front of our house. After I got through I went across the street and cleaned the snow from the sidewalks of a widow lady. A friend passing asked me 'why I did it,' I replied 'why, she's our neighbor'."

We often hear it said that time is wasted in trying to save these newsboys, not perhaps because of the boy himself, but because of that which makes him what he is. It is argued that his environment, the influences which surround him from the day of his birth, will make him a criminal in spite of all we can do.

The Bible holds man responsible.

If you kind reader, believe in God, believe in the Bible, you will find the divine law (Ezekiel XXXIII.) determines your personal responsibility. "So thou, O son of man, I have set thee a watchman unto the house of Israel; therefore thou shalt hear the word at my mouth. If thou dost not speak to warn the wicked from his way, that wicked *man* shall die in his iniquity; but his blood will I require at thy hand. Nevertheless, if thou warn the wicked of his way to turn from it; if he do not turn from his way, he shall die in his iniquity; but thou hast delivered thy soul."

Following down the ages the same responsibility is required of Christians (James IV-17): "To him that knoweth to do good, and doeth it not, to him it is a sin."

The man who fails to rise above the level of his own selfish interests is the man to whom these apply.

The church, at large, today, is like what Napoleon once said: "The army that remains in its entrenchments is beaten." The church remains mostly in its own entrenchments of conventional practices and indifference to the unsaved young men. There is but one remedy for this present indifferent condition, and that is to be found in an awakening of consciousness of personal responsibility for the salvation of the boy.

We need a new doctrine, not a new law, that will bring people back to the Simple Life that demands some self-sacrifice.

If we follow these teachings what shall be our reward?

Do you remember what Pharaoh's daughter said when, winning that strange prize from the bulrushes, on the Nile; she called to the woman whose child might have perished?

Pharaoh's daughter said to the mother: "Take this child away, and nurse it for me, and I will give thee thy wages," and that message is given as the crown of all motherhood on whom the divine mercy falls today. There comes this same message: "Take this child and nurse it for me, and I will pay the thy wages."

The good that you have done you shall know, "not here, but hereafter."

We should never forget that the best and truest lives are those who strew all the years with the sweet aroma of loving and self-sacrificing deeds. Did you ever go, in summer, to the great marshes of our fresh-water lakes, and in the little bayous, where the muck and grasses are so thick it is difficult to even row a boat? If not, it will pay you to go. You find the white water lilies, dotted here and there all over this forsaken waste. They take root and grow silently amid the slime and mud in the quiet waters, until, in mid-summer, they open their creamy beauty to the persuasion of the sunshine, the glory and idealization of all flowers. So amid the lowest and poorest of humanity, among its shadows and mists, we can sow, day by day, our small seeds of gentle and generous deeds, not knowing when they take root, or expecting to ever behold their unfolding into the blossoms on the great river of time.

To have a perfect government we must have a perfect people, and that cannot be accomplished unless we educate, unless we train, our boys in the right direction. If we do our share in this generation it will be easier for those who follow.

The more you mingle among newsboys the easier it is to learn how to influence and guide them in the right path.

They will open out to you a world you have never found, a world full of sunshine. If you are inclined to serve these boys, and are willing to try to teach them how to live right, you will build for yourself a crown of happiness in this world that all the wealth of a nation cannot purchase.

Pastime—the finish.

CHAPTER XXXX.

It is hoped that the preceding pages have given the reader some idea of the workings of Boyville, of the self-governing plan carried on successfully for many years. It has demonstrated the fact, to the president and his faithful associates, the trustees, and the officers of the auxiliaries, that boys can govern themselves, that they can build up and carry on the work that has usually been done by older persons. Corporal punishment is not necessary and no arbitrary authority is needed. There is nothing compulsory about the entire work of the association. The simplest methods are always adopted, keeping in view the wishes of the boy. Not by advanced theories that reach beyond the comprehension of the boy, but by gradually introducing good principles that have a tendency to uplift the boy, and following as nearly as possible the lines he is interested in.

Through the ever-willing assistance of the Humane officers, and later, the splendid work of the Juvenile Court, the association has been able to get behind the cause of much of the wrong-doing of the newsboys, by reaching their parents. Any good physician, to cure a disease, will make every effort possible to discover and cure the cause. There is an old saying: "A stitch in time saves nine." This is certainly true and applicable to work among newsboys. We agree with the many good things said and written by the late Samuel M. Jones, and this in particular: "The only way to help people is to give them an opportunity to help themselves."

Our cities are full of boys growing up to manhood without advice, without help. They are turned aside to do the best they can, to battle with life with everything against them. The question to thinking men today is, shall we permit these boys to continue on the certain road to ruin, or shall we turn a few steps out of our way to lend a helping hand? Shall we wait until they become confirmed criminals and are serving sentences in prisons before we try to help them?

It is much easier to save a soul in a healthy and satisfied, comfortable-feeling body, than in a body wasted by want and with a mind diseased by injustice, cruelty and wrong.

The good accomplished by the members of The Boyville Newsboys' Association, we hope, will go on forever, and that this generation may prove the best and our people continue to be the most prosperous, and our boys grow up to be God-fearing, honest men, is the prayer of every man and woman of our land. But prayers will never be answered if we sit with our hands folded waiting for someone to do the work.

In these hurrying days, when life is becoming complicated in so many ways; when the love of money is greater than the love of mankind, you wonder where can real happiness be found.

Let us kindly suggest a new work, a new field of labor; a field that may test human goodness and human ability, but where you will reap more than riches, more than fame.

Begin today, go out upon the streets, work among the newsboys, reach down to those below, and offer a hand to lift them up. Throw around them the proper protection and influence. In your own city, your own town, at your own doors, are acres of diamonds only waiting for you to help in the work of polishing.

Lector House believes that a society develops through a two-fold approach of continuous learning and adaptation, which is derived from the study of classic literary works spread across the historic timeline of literature records. Therefore, we aim at reviving, repairing and redeveloping all those inaccessible or damaged but historically as well as culturally important literature across subjects so that the future generations may have an opportunity to study and learn from past works to embark upon a journey of creating a better future.

This book is a result of an effort made by Lector House towards making a contribution to the preservation and repair of original ancient works which might hold historical significance to the approach of continuous learning across subjects.

HAPPY READING & LEARNING!

LECTOR HOUSE
LECTOR HOUSE LLP
E-MAIL: lectorpublishing@gmail.com